The Original *Nutcracker* Ballet
–A Hidden Allegory

The Original *Nutcracker* Ballet
–A Hidden Allegory

by
Margaret Fleming-Markarian

Privately Printed
2014

Book design and typesetting: James Wilson
Cover illustration: Margaret Fleming-Markarian

Printed in the United Kingdom by T J International

ISBN:
978-0-9929469-1-3

www.fleming-markarian.co.uk

Contents

Preface

*T*he *Nutcracker* ballet is famous throughout the world today, and it is a great favourite with children at Christmas.
Although much of its original choreography has been lost,
and costume designs and sets have changed with every
new production, the original Tchaikovsky music continues
to be played and to captivate audiences. This music, which
was composed especially for the libretto of *The Nutcracker*,
goes hand in glove with the balletic drama so that, in general, the story has remained the same, in spite of the fact
that it has, since its inception, been criticized as either being
extremely weak, or too complicated to be comprehensible.
Apparently a simple tale about a child's dreamlike adven-
ture with a nutcracker doll which magically turns into a
prince, *The Nutcracker* has, nevertheless, puzzled dance
critics and historians as to why it harbours such enigmatic
imagery. Is it pure imagination or is there a deliberate and
comprehensive meaning which lies at the back of it? This
book examines what is left of the evidence from the ballet's

original production and puts forward possible arguments, based on that evidence, for the understanding of the ballet as an allegory.

Thanks are due to the staff from the following libraries who have assisted me during my research in the compilation of this book: St Petersburg Theatre Library, the British Library and the Royal Academy of Dance Library, London. Thanks are also due to James Wilson, Yulia Vladimirova Knottenbelt and Irina Yatsenko.

Margaret Fleming-Markarian, 2014

List of Plates

Plates 1, 3, 6, 8, 13, 15, 16, 17, 18, 20 and 21 are reproduced courtesy of the St Petersburg Theatre Library. Plates 2, 4, 5, 7, 9, 10, 11, 12, 14 and 19 are illustrations by Bertall reproduced from Alexandre Dumas, *Histoire d'un casse-noisette* (Paris: J Hetzel, 1845). Plate 22 is reproduced from the *Yearbook of the Imperial Theatres, 1892-3* (St Petersburg, 1894). Plate 23 is a sketch by the author from a design by Ivanov photographed in the article 'Casse-Noisette', in *About the House*, vol. 2, no. 8, Christmas 1967, p. 8. Plate 24 is from a sketch by the author.

Introduction

The ballet *Casse-noisette*, known throughout the English-speaking world today as *The Nutcracker*, was first produced at the Maryinsky Theatre in St Petersburg in 1892. Its libretto and costume designs were created by Ivan Vsevolojsky, the then director of the Maryinsky, in collaboration with his ballet master, Marius Petipa, who arranged the scenarios on stage; the ballet's choreography is attributed to Lev Ivanov, assistant ballet master, who took over this task from Petipa, who had fallen ill at the time; the ballet's musical score was composed by Peter Tchaikovsky; and the set designs were created by Mikhail Bocharov and Konstantin Ivanov.[1] Of these original constituent parts of the ballet, the choreography has failed to survive intact, and only a few pieces can be proven to derive from transcriptions recorded before the Russian Revolution of 1917.[2] The bulk of this text relies mainly on original sources other than the choreography.

Occult Symbolism

The libretto of *The Nutcracker* is based on the tale by E T A Hoffmann as translated and adapted by Alexandre Dumas, and published in the mid-1840s.[3] Hoffmann's stories were very influential during the nineteenth century and reflected the taste for the occult which had initially been revived in France, before then spreading throughout Europe. Occultism incorporated a wide range of ideas, including alchemy, cabbala, hermeticism, animal magnetism, dreams, magic, theology and philosophy. As Maria Carlson has commented, this was a time when 'Classics of medieval mysticism, religion and occultism were reprinted. [...] [Moreover,] this huge body of occult material, much of it in French and thus easily accessible to educated Russians, soon found its way into Russia.'[4] Indeed, Tsars Alexander III and Nicholas II were known to sponsor various mystics, spiritualists and occultists, and the Tsarina Alexandra Feodorovna, wife of Nicholas II, was herself very enthusiastic about the occult sciences, magnetism, spiritism and magic.[5] The choice of an occult tale from the works of Hoffmann as the basis for a ballet to be performed in St Petersburg in the early 1890s for the entertainment of the imperial family and their social milieu (who were numerous and staunch supporters of the theatre), was an apt choice.[6] As for the style of presentation, the mode of the day was Symbolism—an aesthetic movement which used symbolic imagery to evoke states of mind and emotions. It had been developed in France in the 1860s and 1870s and was articulated in the 1880s through a series of manifestos; it started to take root as a literary movement in Russia in the 1890s. The Maryinsky Theatre director, Vsevolojsky, a francophile who had been employed at the Russian consulate in Paris (1876-81), would have been familiar with the Symbolist movement. Moreover, the roots of Symbolism lay in early Romanticism, and symbolic imagery had already been a feature incorporated into the Romantic ballet. In addition, Petipa, a Frenchman trained in the French Romantic style, was, by the time of his collaboration with Vsevolojsky, a mature ballet master and expert craftsman.[7] Indeed, the French movement of *le symbolisme* can be viewed as an extension and intensification of Romantic symbolism in general. And its usage within the context of *The Nutcracker* ballet is the same as for other Symbolist art forms, i.e., to evoke an occult world beyond mere natural reality, a world of the imagination. It is the purpose of this text to take the reader on a journey through the ballet's original story and structure (as far as it is possible), in order to elucidate its imaginative, supernatural world and to examine the hidden, allegorical meaning within it.

Act I, Scene I

Nuremberg

The Dumas version of Hoffmann's tale, 'The Nutcracker and the Mouse King', is located in Nuremberg. A free, imperial city of the Holy Roman Empire, Nuremberg had grown rich from overland trade during the Middle Ages, becoming a centre for science and mechanical invention during the Renaissance. However, due to the discovery of new overseas trade routes, Nuremberg's fortunes declined during the sixteenth century. The city began to incur sizeable debts, a situation which led to its being absorbed into the new Kingdom of Bavaria at the signing of the Confederation of the Rhine in 1806.[1] The ballet, through its period costumes, alludes to this date, and through the prominent role of the character of Drosselmayer, who is greatly interested in the mechanisms of clocks and automata, the ballet also alludes to Nuremberg's past history of mechanical invention. Dumas writes that Nuremberg is renowned for its toys, dolls and punchinellos, which are exported to all parts of the world.[2] The Nutcracker doll, around which the whole drama evolves, is, therefore, a typical product of Nuremberg.

The Salon of the Silberhaus Residence

Scene I of the ballet reveals a large salon in the home of the Silberhaus family. The original set design by Konstantin Ivanov presents a Dutch-style, baroque interior, with tiled floor, panelled walls and ceiling.[3] Somewhat incongruously, it does not take after the lighter, baroque style of Catholic Bavaria, but is heavily Protestant in aspect. A tall, Dutch cabinet—perhaps a cabinet of curiosities filled with scientific specimens—stands at the back on the right.[4] A Roman archway, abutted by twin neoclassical pillars, fills the centre back of the stage and frames what looks like a nativity adoration scene, with the Virgin Mary seated with the Christ child on her lap, joined by a group of onlookers who seem just to have arrived, and who are held in wonder at their presence. To the upper right and left of the archway, are scenes of everyday life; to the right is an interior, and to the left a landscape, complete with windmill. The choice of a nativity scene within the setting of the ballet is highly pertinent, as the season is Christmas. But such scenes, whether as paintings on wood panels or even perhaps as Flemish tapestries, all signal that the Silberhaus family are wealthy people, a fact that does not escape Dumas, who takes care to explain that the name 'Silberhaus' itself, means 'house of silver/money'![5] Certainly, the Silberhauses are a well-to-do family, and the porcelain plates and ornaments, which sit on top of the Dutch cabinet, pay further testimony to their status.[6] The panelled ceiling has a tripartite divide, aligning with the tripartite division of the backdrop. To the sides are bold, rectangular designs, compartmentalized into a central lozenge adjoined by triangles touching apex to apex. In the centre are large, eight-pointed stars, formed of two, interlocking squares. These are bold designs, theatrical and occult—lozenges can signify the contact between heaven and earth; [7] whilst triangles aligned horizontally (as they are here), signify the lunar, representing 'the waxing and waning moon, death and life, dying and resurrecting.' [8] As for the motif of the eight-pointed stars, 'its pattern is associated with early astronomy, religion and mysticism. It is symbolic of both stars and humanity's earliest attempts to understand and communicate the order and unity inherent in Creation, nature's rule.' [9] The floor is divided into rows of tiles, parallel to the ceiling divisions, and cut in the shapes of triangles and lozenges. It is as if the 'earth' below (the floor), reflects the 'heaven' above (the ceiling), with the Christ child between earth and heaven (between the floor and ceiling). And the whole scene (we are told in the ballet master's plan) is lit by a single candelabra, which is a symbol of spiritual light. [10] All this possible symbolic import might easily escape an audience's attention; for now, they are merely drawn into a scene of Christmas festivity.

The Christmas Tree is decorated

The ballet's libretto states that: 'The curtain opens onto a large room in the home of President Silberhaus, where the family and their guests are preparing a sumptuously decorated Christmas tree.' [11] Hanging from the tree's branches are gold and silver apples, nuts and confections. [12] At the time of *The Nutcracker* ballet's premiere in St Petersburg in 1892, the tradition of a decorated tree at Christmas had

become established. It was a tradition that originated from
the German states (where fir trees have been known to have
been decorated since the seventeenth century), before eventually taking root in Russia around the time of the marriage
of Princess Charlotte of Prussia to the Emperor Nicholas I in
1817. The custom appears to have stemmed from a belief in
trees that bore fruit at Christmas.

> A writer in 1430 relates that 'not far from Nuremberg
> there stood a wonderful tree. Every year, in the cold-
> est season, on the night of Christ's birth this tree put
> forth blossoms and apples as thick as a man's thumb.
> This in the midst of deep snow and in the teeth of
> cold winds.' [13]

In the libretto's description, this ancient idea of a tree bearing
apples on Christmas Eve is maintained, alongside the nativity scene portrayed on the wall behind. And in the ballet the
tree's apples, detailed as being of gold and silver, thereby take
on the tincture of the sun and the moon. In the occult symbolism of alchemy, the alchemical tree 'bears the fruits of the
sun and moon, gold and silver on each branch.' [14] Indeed, 'the
maturation of the philosopher's stone is represented by the
appearance on the philosophical tree of the fruits of the sun
(gold) and moon (silver).' [15] And so, this decorative detail of
the gold and silver apples would appear to suggest that this
tree is more than just a splendidly decorated tree, and that
it may hold magical and mystical properties associated with
alchemical processes.

The Silberhauses and their Guests

Supervising the festive preparations on stage are Président Silberhaus and his wife. They are brightly and somewhat ostentatiously dressed. The Président appears in knee breeches and tailcoat of grey-and-black stripes, bluebell-blue stockings with dark green-turquoise oval spots, and a waistcoat with turquoise-blue dots; his long hair is in a pigtail fastened to the crown of his head like a tuft. [16] Madame la Président appears in a high-waisted, long gown of bottle green with darker green pinstripes; on her head is a white mob cap tied with an orange-red bow at the front. [17] Their family and the guests who arrive are similarly dressed. [18] Their apparel reflects the style of French fashion which sprang up after the fall of Robespierre in 1794 and was known as 'Les Incroyables et Merveilleuses' (The Unbelievables and Marvellous): it was prevalent during the periods of the Directoire (the Directory) (1795-99) and the Consulat (the Consulate) (1799-1804), and was the mode of the nouveaux riches, especially those who made money by supplying the French armies of the period. It may be that Président Silberhaus, described by Hoffmann simply as 'Medizinalrath' (medical officer) and by Dumas, as 'docteur' (doctor), was in some way, during this epoch, bound up with the supply of medicine for the armies of Napoleon, a supply which was paramount for the success of the Napoleonic military machine. [19] For French Revolutionary armies had come to occupy and become allied with many Germanic states of the Holy Roman Empire in the 1790s; and these states would remain French allies until Napoleon's downfall. Moreover, when Bavaria became a member state of the Confederation of the Rhine in 1806, it was required to provide troops for Napoleon,

and army suppliers to Napoleon's troops, aided by those com-
missioning supplies, were capable of making rapid fortunes.[20]
Perhaps it is also significant of these turbulent times that the
costume designs contain a sketch marked, 'Militia and Lady,'[21]
whose watercolours illustrate military personnel in period uniform, along with a lady. The soldiers are variously dressed in
colours of blue, red and white and different headgear in brown
fur, charcoal black, red and dark turquoise. They would appear
to count themselves among the French ranks, whether French
or allied (German states which opposed Napoleon at this time
were defeated and swallowed up into the lands of other states).
Indeed, in order to secure a hold on territory and its wealth, an
alliance with the Napoleonic cause was necessary for German
princelings. And here, albeit in a domestic setting, this necessary diplomatic *entente cordiale* between peoples is hinted
at by the presence of the military, and the status of Président
Silberhaus and his family is somehow bound up with it. More
enigmatically, however, on the same costume design page as
the soldiers, is a lady with a brown umbrella.

The lady carrying a brown umbrella is dressed in a long,
white gown with a laurel wreath-patterned surround at the
hem, shoulder jacket of red with dark-brown fur trim and
a red and brown bonnet plumed with brown and white
feathers. The laurel wreath, associated with the crowning of
victors in Graeco-Roman times, stands out immediately in
this ensemble, as it was a motif common to the ornamental
vocabulary of the Napoleonic era. For Napoleon saw himself
as a victor and notably had himself portrayed in his imperial
regalia, wearing a golden laurel wreath of victory, in an 1806
oil painting by Ingres.[22] Indeed, the very wearing by others of

the laurel wreath symbol would signal support for Napoleon. The other outstanding feature of the lady's appearance is, of course, the brown umbrella which she carries. Umbrellas began to be popularized by French women in the seventeenth century, a trend which continued in the eighteenth century, gradually spreading out into general use. [23] Maybe this lady *is* a French lady. She is almost certainly a guest, but she is not identified specifically in the Stepanov choreographic score. [24] However, there is mention of a female guest who attracts the attention of the Président Silberhaus and his wife. 'Silberhaus asks his wife: "You invited her too?" To which she replies, "No, she came herself—what can we do?" ' [25] It seems likely that the lady with the umbrella could be this same 'uninvited' guest, who would not have needed her umbrella if she had prearranged, on account of having received a prior invitation, to come by cab. But there is innuendo in this tête-à-tête between Silberhaus and his wife. If this lady is a French lady of wealth and even political standing (she is certainly dressed well and the umbrella *is* a recognized symbol of power, although in this case, denoting earthly power as it is brown) and she is acquainted with the Silberhauses, then, in those days, it would have been undiplomatic, even politically impossible, to turn her away. Nonetheless, in this passing of remarks between husband and wife, there is insinuated an underlying discord between the French and the Bavarians.

The Clock strikes Nine and the Christmas Tree is illuminated

As the decoration of the Christmas tree is nearing completion, 'the clock strikes nine. At each stroke, the owl [guarding the clock] flaps his wings'. [26] This flapping is easy to connect to the common expression 'time flies', a translation of the Latin phrase *tempus fugit*. Generally speaking, its intended sense is '"Time's a-wasting". As such, it expresses concern that one's limited time [on earth] is being consumed by nothing in particular or by something which may have little intrinsic substance, importance, or urgency'. [27] This thought is occultly applicable to the huge display of wealth in view, inferring maybe that materiality, no matter how grand, is as fleeting as time. Moreover, the owl itself is a symbol of knowledge, i.e., rational knowledge as opposed to intuitive knowledge, and therefore its attachment to the clock with its mechanical workings, lends more substance to this concept of temporal time in relation to the physical world. [28] But there is hardly a moment for an audience to contemplate this strange clock, for no sooner has it chimed, than it is time to call in the children. [29] The tree is nearly ready, and soon it lights up brilliantly 'as if by magic', accompanied by a scintillating *accelerando* over eight bars, starting *piano* and gradually becoming *fortissimo*. [30] This 'magical' effect was no doubt contrived using electric light which began to be installed in St Petersburg in the 1880s, and it must have been impressive then. [31] From a symbolic and traditional point of view, this illumination metamorphoses the tree into the 'Tree of Light [...] the tree of rebirth, [...] the Christian Christmas Tree and the Teutonic fir tree of Woden'. [32]

With the tree lit, the door to the salon swings open, and, according to the Dumas text, Marie (Claire) and Fritz, the children of the Silberhauses, and their friends, are ushered in by their governess. [33] In the published libretto, however, the children are led in by Silberhaus's niece, Marianne. It would seem therefore, that Marianne and the governess are one and the same in the ballet.[34] An early photograph of Marianne with Claire and Fritz, shows her in a high-waisted, white gown and whitish cap similar in shape to a Phrygian cap.[35] The Bertall illustration in the Dumas text, on the other hand, depicts the governess as an old woman in a modest, dark gown and long, white apron: her head is covered by a simple scarf.[36] This depiction of a governess, with an outwardly dull appearance, has been deliberately passed over in favour of introducing into the ballet the more appealing stage presence of a young, fashionably dressed Marianne. The choice of her name 'Marianne' is significant too, as it resonates with 'Marianne', the symbol of the French Republic and a personification of liberty and reason, which became popular from the 1790s.[37] Attributes of Marianne include the Phrygian cap of liberty. Might there be some occult inference here, that one of Marianne's tasks is to instil the principles of the day—liberty and reason—into the children?

'At the sight of the tree, the children, astonished, are stopped in their tracks.'[38]

In the Dumas text, the lead-in to the Christmas tree commences at the salon door, where Fritz and Marie (Claire) are met by their parents who take them by the hand.[39]

'Come, my little ones,' they say, 'and see what the Infant Jesus has just brought you.' [...] When they entered the salon [...] they beheld the Christmas tree [...] fully laden with [...] golden apples, sugar flowers [...] sugar-coated almonds [...] and everything is sparkling from the lights of a hundred candles hidden in its foliage.[40]

In the minds of the Silberhauses, the candle-lit tree, with its bounty of fruits and sweets, is clearly envisioned as a gift from the Christ Child—and this connection is implicit in Ivanov's original set design for the opening scene (see above), which has a painting of the nativity scene centrally placed on the backdrop, behind where the tree would stand.[41] Dumas continues: 'Catching sight of the tree, Fritz executes several *entrechats* [i.e., he jumps up and down] [...] whilst Marie [Claire] did not even try to hold back two large tears of joy, which, like liquid pearls, rolled down her illuminated face, as on a rose in May.' Thus, the Silberhaus children react differently—Fritz shows his emotions outwardly, leaping into the air, while Claire has a very different, inward reaction, made visible only by a couple of tears which roll down her cheeks. It is as if, as evidenced by her joyous face, she has experienced a vision triggered by the brilliance before her. In her case one can imply that the 'gift of the Infant Jesus' (known in Christianity as the 'Light of the World'), rather than the tree itself, *is* the light emanating from the tree—a light that symbolizes divine truth. However, if she is moved by some vision, this would be difficult to portray solely from the child's facial expression, at a distance on stage. Nevertheless, the audience must surely empathize with both children, as they themselves take in the candle-bedecked tree's sparkling spectacle.

Claire and Fritz, and their Friends receive Gifts

The original costume design for Claire shows a child with golden locks in a high-waisted, white gown with a double frill at the hem, and a sash of golden-yellow around her waist and tied at the back.[42] She wears long, white evening gloves and white stockings, and on her feet are golden-yellow slippers with sharply pointed toes. Her apparel of white and gold, both symbolic of light, synchronize with the name Claire, which itself means 'light'. She is sketched alongside four friends, all of whom are, to a greater or lesser extent, more fancily dressed than Claire with garish patterns, bonnets and bows, ruffles and aprons. Claire, in contrast, is plain. This plainness originates in the Bertall illustrations of the Dumas text.[43] Here, Marie (Claire) is also in a plain, white dress, made even plainer by the absence of a sash. But more significantly, the waistline is not high, as in the ballet design, but fitted into the waist, signalling the fashion of an earlier epoch in the eighteenth century. Although, as it will be seen below, Vsevolojsky must have taken note of Bertall's illustrations, this difference in style between the Bertall illustrations and Vsevolojsky's costume sketches is consistent, providing circumstantial evidence that the choice of the Napoleonic era was deliberate.

The costume design for Fritz shows a child with short, light-brown hair in a trouser suit of sky blue with a broad, white collar and white cuffs, both fringed at the edges. He wears white stockings and dull-black, pointed shoes.[44] The name 'Fritz' is a diminutive of Frederick and means 'peaceful ruler'. In view of Fritz's future behaviour in the ballet, this appellation does not blend with his character. However, if one relates his name to Frederick the Great, the warring king of Prussia, then one can view Fritz much more suitably, as taking after him.[45] Certainly, in the Dumas text, Fritz is portrayed as having an interest in toy soldiers and is illustrated playing with them. [46] In the ballet's original costume design, Fritz is, like Claire, sketched alongside his friends, who are similarly clothed.

As the children stand in front of the tree, enraptured by its spectacle, Silberhaus orders a march to be played. [47] During the march, all the children line up and 'each child receives gifts along with a party novelty and a dressing-up costume. The children dress up playfully.' [48] At the close of the march, they break into a short, fast gallop which finishes with a loud *crescendo*. A reviewer of the premiere remarked that the youngsters 'receive the gifts very naturally and with animation, and dance a gallop holding their gifts pleasingly.' [49] They are clearly overjoyed with their presents. At the end of the gallop, the general liveliness grows apace with the entrance of parents and guests dressed as 'incroyables', and they too dance. Included in their number, is, according to the same reviewer, 'Miss Petipa, [who] with great style, makes much ado with her lorgnette and the train of her dress.' [50] It is unclear whether the 'Miss Petipa' here is 'Marie' or 'Vera' Petipa (both daughters of the ballet master Marius Petipa), but the costume designs show the same sketch designated for them both. [51] Again there is a lady in a high-waisted dress, but instead of plain white, the bodice is red, there is a sash of pink, and the long skirt is adorned with gold stars (two banks of three rows), and gold foliage around the hem. She wears gold-laced sandals, long white gloves with gold stars and a pink shawl. This outfit demonstrates admirably the taste for French luxury fashions which had spread with Napoleonic conquest. Moreover, gold stars appeared on many fashionable objets d'art of the day.

But, more pertinently, the presence of red with gold stars on this dress signals the gold stars on a red ground which made up the coat of arms of the Bonaparte family before Napoleon became emperor in 1804. Undoubtedly, this fashionable lady is meant to reflect Bonapartist sympathies in the Bavarian states—she may even, in some manner, be individually connected to the Bonaparte family. [52] As for the lorgnette (eyeglasses held on a stick), which Miss Petipa is deemed to make much ado with, well, that was all part of the affectation of the fashion of the 'incroyables' whose outlook is hinted at here, i.e., as being as narrow as the view given by the lorgnette itself! Indeed, all the costumes of the grown-ups who dance as 'incroyables' and 'merveilleuses' are described by a reviewer as 'whimsical costumes of the French Revolution.' [53] As the dancing concludes, the godfather to Claire, *conseiller* Drosselmayer, arrives.

Godfather Drosselmayer

'On the last stroke on the half hour of the clock, Drosselmayer enters the salon.' [54] According to the Dumas version of the Hoffmann story, Drosselmayer is a 'conseiller de médecine', a medical advisor or doctor. [55] However, Dumas goes on to explain that, unlike other doctors, Drosselmayer was very interested in mechanics and mechanical objects, such as clocks, and he liked to mend them if they failed to function properly. [56] It is, moreover, appropriate that Drosselmayer's name is composed of two parts—'Drossel' which is used in German in conjunction with types of mechanical valve, and 'mayer' which derives from the Middle High German word 'meiger' meaning 'higher' or 'superior.' [57] The name therefore would appear to harbour an occult inference that Drosselmayer is some sort of advanced mechanic. In the costume designs, a tall, thin man is portrayed, in brown breeches and long, brown kaftan, typical of the type worn by Russian merchants. [58] His shirt is white with frilled jabot; his waistcoat is pale yellow; his stockings are grey, and he wears buckled, black, pointed shoes. He holds a stick in his right hand. On his head is a grey-white perruque under which is slung a black strap, which supports an eyepatch covering up his right eye. This oddity is compounded with a pointed nose and chin, and a large, left eye which stares out. Vsevolojsky's rendering of Drosselmayer is very similar to Bertall's illustration of him. [59] His general appearance is that of an eighteenth-century gentleman and certainly not that of an 'incroyable'. As for his complexion, Dumas records that 'he had a wrinkled face like a rennet apple which had suffered an April frost', a characteristic that is shared by both the theatre design and the original illustration in the Dumas text. [60] On catching sight of Drosselmayer, 'The children go and hide beside their parents'.[61] They are, presumably, frightened by his freakish appearance. When, however, they see that he has brought them toys, they calm down.

Silberhaus and Drosselmayer partake of Snuff

Silberhaus, seeing Drosselmayer enter the salon, moves forward to greet him and offers him snuff from his snuff box.

By the eighteenth century, snuff had become popular among the upper echelons of society and Napoleon himself partook of snuff. [62] The boxes containing the snuff were often made of gold and encrusted with jewels. Indeed, they were a sight to be seen and an elaborate etiquette attached itself to the presentation of the snuff in its beautiful box.

A French pamphlet of *c.* 1750 [...] lists fourteen movements:

1) Take the box in the right hand
2) Pass it to the left hand
3) Tap it
4) Open it
5) Present it to the company
6) Retract it
7) Always keep it open
8) Tap on the sides to heap the snuff in the middle
9) Take a clean pinch in your right hand
10) Hold for sometime before taking to the nose
11) Take to the nose
12) Sniff judiciously with both nostrils and without grimacing
13) Sneeze, cough and spit
14) Close the snuff box. [63]

In contrast to the above elaborate etiquette, the dialogue and instruction in the original choreographic score in Stepanov of the giving and handing back of Silberhaus's snuff box is minimal. 'Silberhaus says: "You don't mean to say you've forgotten your old habit, snuff!" and he holds out his snuff box and Drosselmayer gives it back, and both partake of snuff from their hands and sniff'. [64] But one suspects that there is here, as the prescription above of the etiquette suggests,

a more detailed manner of delivery written into this passing moment, a moment which seems to be trivial, but is so
telling of those who take part in it. Silberhaus is, in effect,
showing off his snuff box, like a miniature, bejewelled toy but
for adults, a hugely expensive version of the trinkets already
received by the children as Christmas presents. [65]

The Cauliflower and the Pie

In Tchaikovsky's piano reduction of *Casse-noisette*, it states:
'The two Silberhaus children wait impatiently for godfather Drosselmayer's presents to be distributed. He has two
crates brought in: from one, he pulls out a large cauliflower
and from the other, a large pie. Everyone is astounded.' [66] In
Petipa's scenario, it states more specifically: 'Drosselmayer
has two crates brought in: from one, he extracts a large head
of cauliflower—it is a gift for Clara; from the other, a large
pie—it is for Fritz.' [67]

The symbolism of the cauliflower and the pie are not generally recognizable today, but they almost inevitably relate here
to 'the "great supper" [...] eaten by Christians on Christmas
eve. [...] The great supper traditionally consists of seven small
main dishes, eaten before the midnight service made up from
white vegetables, one of which is always, but always, cauliflower, white fishes and eggs and they symbolise the seven
sufferings of the Virgin.' [68] As the cauliflower is Claire's gift,
one can then, in the light of this connection with the Virgin,
reference her white dress in the costume designs to that of
the traditional white dress of the Virgin. Certainly, the caring
qualities attributed to the Virgin, are soon to become emi-
nently visible in Claire's behaviour. As for the symbolism of

the pie (in the original French, 'pâté'), it must represent one of the remaining Christmas Eve dishes. And as for the meaning of the word 'pâté', it can refer to a pastry or a pie. It derives its meaning from paste, pasta or batter. The phrase in French, 'tous les hommes sont faits de la même pâté', literally means, 'all men are made from the same paste.' In this context, the pastry or pie can be seen to symbolize earthly matter. Because the pie is Fritz's gift, one can then relate the idea of earthy matter to Fritz's character and his appetite for life, which will become more apparent as the ballet progresses. But at this juncture, for the children, both the cauliflower and the pie appear rather uninteresting presents, and they seem disappointed. Notwithstanding, 'Drosselmayer smiles and orders the gifts to be brought before him. [...] He starts them [life-size mechanical dolls] up with a key. [...] To the great joy of the children, a large doll emerges out of the cauliflower head and from the pie—a soldier.'[69]

The Sutler and the Soldier

The doll which emerges from the cauliflower, is described as a sutler, (one who is authorized to follow an army, and sell goods and provisions to the soldiers).[70] In the costume designs, she is dressed in the colours of the Bavarian army, the cornflower blue and white of the ruling house of the Wittelsbachs.[71] She wears a cornflower-blue jacket with turned-back lapels of white with gold buttons, a long white waistcoat underneath (also with gold buttons), which covers the top part of a white hooped skirt to just below knee height. There is also a broad band of cornflower blue surrounding the lower skirt, edged in gold and with a gold trefoil pattern going round its upper edge. On her head, over a perruque, is a gold and silver helmet with horsehair, caterpillar crest; on her feet are black pointed shoes and long dark-grey gaiters. In her right outstretched hand, she holds a riding whip, marked alongside as 'cravache'. Her left hand rests on her waist, adding a slight swagger to her pose. The Soldier doll which emerges from the pie, on the other hand, is designated 'conscrit avec fusil' (conscript with rifle), although there is no rifle drawn.[72] He too is dressed in the cornflower blue and white of the Wittelsbachs, and his uniform is similar in style to the girl's. He wears white breeches, a cornflower-blue jacket to the waist with turned-back white lapels, and the same black pointed shoes and long dark-grey gaiters. He too has a perruque, but on top sits a tall cornflower-blue tubular hat, peaked at the front and at the back, and with a broad white band around the foot. Gold buttons on the peaks match those on his waistcoat.

Both the Sutler and the conscript dolls are in very swish military uniforms of Bavarian cornflower blue and white, and this appearance alone would indicate that they are meant to date from the accession of Maximilian Joseph as Prince-Elector of Bavaria in 1799.[73] For, before that date, the army had been much run-down and the procurement of supplies had been very inadequate. However, shortly after Maximilian Joseph's accession, improvements were made to the military and it was then that the traditional cornflower blue was reintroduced for infantry uniforms. The Raupenhelm helmet with fore-and-aft horsehair plume (which the Sutler wears, and which became characteristic of the Bavarian army) was brought in at the same time. Interestingly, the army's organization, including its medical services, was also modernized during this period, which might explain Drosselmayer's choice of doll, given that he is, in the Dumas text, designated a medical advisor/doctor by profession. It is interesting too that Maximilian Joseph not only stopped the purchase of officers' commissions, but introduced general conscription in 1804. If the soldier in the designs described as a 'conscrit', refers to this conscription, then the date of the drama moves forward at least to 1804, the year when Napoleon, as First Consul, became Emperor.[74] Maximilian Joseph was at this time allied to the French, and the reorganization of his army relied on borrowing from the French model. The 'conscrit' we have here in *The Nutcracker* reflects such borrowings in the Bavarian artillery; and the Sutler who holds a horse whip makes reference to the reintroduction of the light (or horse) artillery.[75]

Automata

Drosselmayer's dolls are, in effect, life-size automata, mechanical devices that were often made in the image of people and animals, and that imitated their natural movements. During the eighteenth century, automata developed to a highly sophisticated level and were not only commissioned by the very wealthy, but went on show in salons, as well as at market fairs.[76] If, in the ballet, Drosselmayer is actually bestowing this pair of mechanical dolls, as well as the succeeding pair, as gifts for the children, then it is certain that he must have been very rich, or, alternatively, given his interest in clocks and their mechanisms, he may have constructed them himself! Dumas writes that Drosselmayer had, by dint of studying human mechanics, become an expert in spring mechanisms from which he 'used to construct men who marched, saluted, fenced; women who danced, played the harpsichord, the harp and the viol'.[77] Furthermore, Dumas notes that Drosselmayer's perruque is made of glass (which equates to Hoffmanns's original description of Drosselmayer), a sure sign of the clear headedness of the man. And both Hoffmann and Dumas garb Drosselmayer in a yellow frock-coat.[78] Yellow is the colour of light; and light, especially as a sun image, was the favourite metaphor of the eighteenth century, a period known as the European Enlightenment, and a movement which brought light (in the form of reason and knowledge) in order to drive out the darkness (of unknowing and superstition).[79] From this standpoint, it is unclear in the ballet so far as to why Vsevolojsky should have chosen to sketch Drosselmayer in a *brown* kaftan, as opposed to a *yellow* kaftan. On the other hand, it is rather more obvious, as to why the automata are military personnel. Indeed, the precision of the mechanical movements of the automata mimic the precise drill-like movements that soldiers would learn, especially at this time when armies were becoming more disciplined. In addition, the human body itself was beginning to be seen as a machine. De La Mettrie wrote in the mid-eighteenth century, 'The human body is a machine which winds its own springs. It is the living image of perpetual movement. Nourishment keeps up the movement which fever excites. Without food, the soul pines away, goes mad, and dies exhausted'.[80] Indeed, with the promotion of science and the growth of scientific academies towards the end of the eighteenth century in Europe, religious and metaphysical thought diminished. It was generally considered that:

The dismissal of metaphysics from the realm of analysis elevated rigor, deductive mathematics, and formal precision over equivocation, arbitrariness, and imagination, all the latter being commonly linked to the feminine.[81]

Moreover,

The development of antimetaphysical analysis was intertwined with the elevation of rigorous and systematic rationality. By the time of the French Revolution, this analytic rationality was also clearly associated with masculinity.[82]

Overall, Drosselmayer and his automata are caricatures of their age and its interest in science and reason, as masculine pursuits.

Harlequin and Columbine

Claire and Fritz are captivated by the automata and are granted permission to stay up till ten o'clock. Then, 'Drosselmayer has two large snuff boxes brought in, out of which appear a harlequin and columbine (a devil and she-devil). [...] Demonic dance of the wound-up dolls.'[83]

In the original costume designs, Harlequin is dressed in a jacket, breeches, and stockings, all in a traditional *commedia dell' arte* pattern of diamond-shaped lozenges of light purple and white.[84] On his feet are light-purple pointed shoes. His upper face is traditionally masked in black; around his neck is a white ruff, and on his head is a metallic-coloured bicorn hat. He brandishes a large club. Columbine is dressed in a stylish outfit which matches that of Harlequin in colour and pattern, but with the addition of a purple-and-white striped bodice and stockings.[85] She too wears purple pointed shoes and a bicorn hat, but in her case, with a large purple flower on the hat's front facing. She wears charcoal gauntlets and brandishes a short, thin baton. The couple (who in the *commedia dell' arte* are inseparable companions) are placed on the page facing each other, batons aloft, as if they are about to take a swipe at each other.[86]

The bicorn hats which the couple wear were adopted by European military officers in the 1790s and are readily associated with Napoleon who wore one himself. The *commedia dell' arte* characters, on the other hand, are, of course, of Italian origin, and their donning of bicorn hats may imply a reference to Napoleon's victorious Italian campaigns of the late 1790s and early 1800s, and, in particular, to the city of Venice, which ceded to Napoleon in 1797.[87] And perhaps it is to Venice that this pair belong. After all, Venice used to celebrate Carnival with masked balls up until 1797, which included masked costumes from the *commedia dell' arte*.[88] But, more pertinently, Venice was famous for its Tyrian dyes, especially those of purple; and maybe it is *this* purple (which finds itself on the costumes of Harlequin and Columbine) which marks them out as inhabitants of that city. But, in any event, Napoleon took control over the Italian states and established national conscription there. Careful regard was paid to those conscripted, and men who were cobblers, weavers, dressmakers, tailors or gunsmiths were given preference.[89] These categories do not, of course, pertain to theatre players like Harlequin and Columbine. However, the designs do show the couple in militant mood, and a harlequin was known to have 'sometimes lashed into a frenzy of madness'. [90] Perhaps they are simply meant to be volunteers in the Italian army, many of whom entered service between 1796 and 1802. Although volunteers represented only a fraction of the men serving in Napoleon's Italian army, they were, nevertheless, considered to be 'the solid foundation upon which the army was constructed'. [91] Moreover, conscripts 'were often led by officers and N.C.O.s who volunteered'. [92] And here note has to be taken of the fact that officers wore bicorn hats, hats which Harlequin and Columbine also wear. In addition, it cannot be denied that, historically, the Italian army under the Napoleonic regime played a role in the development of an Italian national consciousness; and the same could be said for Bavarian consciousness and the role played by the Bavarian army under the Elector Maximilian Joseph.

The idea for Harlequin seems to have arisen from Hoffmann's harlequins which formed part of the motley troops lined up against the army of mice later in the story. [93] In the Dumas version, the harlequins are replaced by a 'Sergent Arlequin' (Sergeant Harlequin), who leads twenty men into battle against the army of mice. [94] This harlequin, as a sergeant, is therefore an officer and, in the Bertall illustrations, he does wear a modest bicorn hat. [95]

The libretto continues: 'Having been wound up, the dolls begin to move, turn and dance; the children are thrilled, but Silberhaus, fearing for the safety of the expensive presents, orders them to be carried off into the cabinet'. [96] However, 'Claire and Fritz are now enchanted and wish to keep the

toys. The parents forbid this. Claire cries. Fritz throws a tan-
trum. In order to console them, Drosselmayer pulls out of
his pocket a third present—a nutcracker.'[97]

The Nutcracker

The Nutcracker doll is shown twice in the costume designs:
it appears in the sketch of Drosselmayer, lodged in the left-
hand pocket of his kaftan, with its head and handle poking
out; and it also appears separately as a fellow in a fur-lined
purple coat with corded toggles, white breeches and black
boots.[98] He has a large beak nose, large eyes, a large red
mouth and a jutting jaw with a short white beard. His dark
hair is short and curly, sprouting out behind from beneath a
bright-red cap. At the back of his neck is attached the wooden
handle which operates the Nutcracker's mouth movements
when it opens and shuts to crack the nuts. In the Hoffmann
account it is stated that his light-green eyes 'spoke nothing
but friendship and benevolence.'[99] In the Dumas account it
is stated that his appearance indicates 'a man of education
and taste.'[100] And that appearance (which corresponds to
the ballet costume design) details his jacket as 'a Polish coat
in purple velvet, with frogging and buttons of gold.'[101] His
hat, however, is 'strangely, for one having a superior taste
in clothes, a small, badly-made mountain dweller's cap.'[102]
Neither Hoffmann nor Dumas remark on the Nutcracker's
cap as being of a bright-red hue. But it is the red colouring
of the cap in the costume designs that immediately flags up
a 'bonnet rouge', that Phrygian cap in red which so typified
revolutionary France from the 1790s, and which symbolized liberty.[103] Is the red Nutcracker's cap meant to signal

an alliance with revolutionary France? perhaps also relating to Polish troops who, like the Italians, fought in the French armies of Napoleon? [104] Or is this an occult and risqué hint at the desire for freedom among Poles at the time of the ballet in 1892, when Poland was partitioned between Russia, Prussia and Austria? [105] Of course the sheer excellence of the Polish velvet jacket worn by the Nutcracker is evidence which, according to Dumas, shows the Nutcracker to be a man of taste and education. [106] He is, de facto, an attractive man, but Claire is more than attracted to the Nutcracker: she is *captivated* by him.

> Claire asks the *conseiller* [Drosselmayer] what the Nutcracker is for: he takes a nut and makes the Nutcracker crack it. Fritz, hearing the 'knak-knak' of the Nutcracker, becomes interested in it. He wants to have a turn at cracking nuts. Claire does not want to give the Nutcracker to him. The parents make it clear to the little girl that the Nutcracker does not belong to her alone. Claire hands over her favourite gift to her brother and looks on in dread, as Fritz cracks two nuts, then he sticks such a large nut into the Nutcracker's mouth, that the teeth break. [107]

Through Drosselmayer's demonstration, the purpose of the Nutcracker is made clear to Claire: it cracks the nuts and liberates the seeds within. Symbolically, seeds are said to represent 'latent, non-manifest forces' that drive reproduction, the alternating cycle of life and death. [108] Certainly, in Germany, nuts placed in tombs were 'emblematic of regeneration and immortality. Searches in the old tombs of Wurtemburg [...] always [found] a number of nuts.'[109] Could the humble Nutcracker, a toy gadget for a child, be regarded as a key mover in such a regenerative process on a more cosmic scale? Its symbolism will gather moss as the drama develops. But, for now, it is just a broken object. 'Fritz, laughing, throws the toy away. Claire picks him up and caressing him, tries to console him. She picks up a doll from its bed, and lays down the good-natured Nutcracker in its place.'[110] Evidently, Claire views the Nutcracker as, at the very least, an object to be cared for; whilst Fritz views the Nutcracker as a mechanism which, to his amusement, failed to function when its teeth were smashed. A lullaby (*berceuse*) follows—a beautiful rocking 2/4 tune, during which Claire cradles the injured Nutcracker and makes threatening gestures to those who might mean harm.[111] In spite of her warning, she is rudely interrupted twice (lasting eight bars at a time) by Fritz and his friends with their din of drums and trumpets.[112] Thereby, the sweet calm of the *berceuse* is juxtaposed with the raucous, hostile actions of the boys, a miniature soundscape of peace, interjected by war. After the second interruption, the piano reduction states: 'To cut short this tumult, the Président invites his guests to dance a Gross-Vater.'[113]

The Gross-Vater Dance

The Gross-Vater dance (literally, 'Grandfather dance') is a traditional German folk tune from the seventeenth century, which was played at the end of weddings and became known as the 'Kehraus' (literally, 'sweep-out'). Here in the ballet, however, the playing of the Gross-Vater dance signals the close of the evening. It is a processional dance, with young and old processing round the room. The first verse reads as follows:

> When grandfather married grandmother
> Grandfather was then the groom
> And grandmother was the bride
> The pair were bound in marriage
> Who knows, how that is now
> Who knows, what there is still to come. [114]

These words look back to the hopes and fears that surround a new marriage, and would, for those remembering them, no doubt bring back sentimental memories. The following verses were written later and relate to the historical, German setting of the ballet. [115] The second verse is as follows:

> When grandfather married grandmother
> No-one then, addressed a woman as 'Mamsell'
>   or 'Madam'
> The demure young lady, and the housewife
> Were truly German in body and soul.

Straight away, one can feel a resentment for the French terms of address to women, brought into German etiquette by Napoleonic influences, and the writer looks back to a time when women were purely German. The third verse continues:

When grandfather married grandmother
A moral modesty still reigned then
One dressed most respectably and found it
    unsightly
To go along the streets in Grecian nudity.

This verse criticizes the fashions of 'Les Incroyables et Merveilleuses' (a term which is specified in the costume designs for *The Nutcracker*). The words refer to the making of Grecian-styled dresses of this mode which either did not cover up parts of the body, or, by the use of diaphanous materials, immodestly and outrageously revealed nude body parts underneath. This verse is testimony to the fact that wherever Napoleon's armies went, French fashions followed. The fourth verse continues:

When grandfather married grandmother
Keeping house was not then disapproved of
She [the wife] didn't read novels, she did the
    cooking
And her child meant more to her than a lapdog.

In this verse, the traditional domestic, active family role of the wife is valued over pastimes such as reading novels and spending time with house dogs instead of attending to one's children. It hints at the life of luxury for those women benefitting from the fortunes of nouveaux riches Germans who had benefited from their alliance with the Napoleonic cause. The fifth verse continues:

When grandfather married grandmother
At that time, when one received a man of honour
A handshake for every noteworthy occasion
Was worth more than an oath today.

Criticism in this verse extends to male morality, looking
back to a time when men were men of their word, and deals
were sealed with a shake of the hand. It insinuates that codes
of conduct have now lost their worth. The sixth verse reverts
to the role of women:

When grandfather married grandmother
At that time self-interest was tethered and tame
She [grandmother] did not break the bonds
    of reserve
Like an all devouring lion of today.

The text here hints at the greed of the Napoleonic period
for luxurious goods, for which there was a thriving market
fuelled by those who had made new fortunes and who could
afford them. The seventh verse continues:

When grandfather married grandmother
Man's energy then was still not useless
Effeminate daintiness, the cowardly dreamer
Was mocked and despised by women.

The French cultural influence of 'les incroyables' is here
berated as effeminate, as opposed to a more traditional man-
ly German culture. The final verse sums up:

When grandfather married grandmother
The patriot did not then despair
O, give to the Germans the sweet prospect
Of a return to the happy days of grandfather.

This final verse looks back nostalgically to a golden age
before the era of Napoleon, and it is telling that all the verses (bar the first) were written in 1812, for that is the year
of Napoleon's defeat in Russia, and when many German intellectuals, appalled by the terror and atheism of the French
Revolution, had begun to look back to native German traditions, uncontaminated by foreign influences. But Bavarian
conscripts, at this point, were still fighting on the side of
Napoleon against Russia.[116] Indeed, Bavarians were fighting in the French army under Gouvion Saint-Cyr and took
part in the first and second battles of Polotsk of 1812 against
Russian forces, after which they were defeated and largely
destroyed.[117] This unfortunate 'German' memory was obviously not the memory associated with the Gross-Vater tune,
which, according to a reviewer at the ballet's premiere, 'probably started the hearts a-beating of older members of the
audience with recollections of long-past youth'.[118] It is likely that the audience members with memories of traditional
German folk music were, in fact, Germans themselves, hail-
ing from the German colonies in Russia established between
1765 and 1819, the most notable of which was to be found
in St Petersburg.[119] Many Germans had arrived during the
reign of Catherine II (1762-96), who was herself German
by birth. Indeed, the colonists had become established in
Russian society and had taken up high positions. This is

extremely relevant to the year of 1812, when Count Peter Christianovich Wittgenstein, a major general of German descent, successfully commanded the right wing of the Russian army in the first and second battles of Polotsk. Indeed, it was his victory at the second battle of Polotsk that decided the fate of St Petersburg and earned him the title of 'Saviour of St Petersburg', for, following defeat here, Napoleon then turned his attentions to the taking of Moscow. [120] Therefore those of German origin living in St Petersburg and its surroundings certainly had much to be proud of vis-à-vis their adoptive country of Russia and its encounter with Napoleon. And, no doubt, the old traditional folk tune of Gross-Vater, with its defiant words against the invasive French culture of the Napoleonic era, evoked memories of their German heritage, as well as the role played by Wittgenstein, one of their own, in saving the city of St Petersburg from French attack.

The Evening comes to a Close

Following the Gross-Vater dance, the guests take their leave of the Président and his wife. Their number includes Drosselmayer, who repeats the etiquette of snuff taking. As everyone departs, a footman follows in their train, carrying out the candelabra. [121] 'The children are ordered off to bed. Claire asks permission to take the ill Nutcracker with her. The parents refuse. She goes off very despondently, after having wrapped up her dear one'. [122] When the room is at last empty, the music changes from an *allegro semplice* to a *moderato con moto*. 'The stage is bare. Night has fallen. The moon illuminates the salon through the window'. [123] And so, the scene is transformed from a brightly-lit picture of worldly endeavour, to a mysterious, otherworldly environment, silvered by moonlight. Indeed, it is the moonlight itself which now gives another meaning to the word 'Silberhaus' which, hitherto translated as 'house of money', can also be rendered more literally as 'house of silver' or 'silvered house'. The silver component takes on lunar qualities associated with purity, even virginal purity, such as can be associated with the young Claire herself. Moreover, silver is seen here as silvered light, and the name 'Claire' means, as mentioned above, 'light'. Indeed, silver

> is pure light such as passes unsullied through transparent crystal, clear water, the reflection of a mirror or the flashing of a diamond. It is like clear conscience, pure intent, open-heartedness, fair dealing. It summons faithfulness in its footsteps. [124]

And so, the pure clear light of the moon, emanating far from the earth and untouched by humankind, replaces and contrasts with the man-made light of the candelabra, which is removed manually from the scene. The strength of the moonlight is weak in comparison with sunlight; but it is enough to reveal Claire, who cautiously returns in her night clothes, wishing to see her beloved Nutcracker before retiring to bed. 'She is fearful. She approaches the bed of the Nutcracker who seems to emanate a supernatural light'. [125]

Claire is mesmerized

It is evident that Claire's attention has been completely captured by the Nutcracker doll. She is, so to speak, 'mesmerized'; and, during the epoch in which the ballet is set, 'mesmerism' was certainly taken seriously. Originally called 'animal magnetism', mesmerism could be induced by one body in another at a distance. [126] 'The mesmeric influence operates invisibly, without contact, and without hindrance from intervening obstacles, so that a person may be sent into a mesmeric state by one operating upon him at distance, or in a different room.' [127] The operator controls the thoughts and desires of the person influenced by sending out an 'electro-nervous fluid', and, in the case of a somnambulist (which Claire could be considered as here), controls their movements too. [128] Moreover, in a state of mesmeric trance, clairvoyance can occur, with ideas being supplied by the mesmerizer. [129] Taking on board this supposition that Claire could now be sleepwalking in some kind of 'clair-voyant', i.e. 'clear-seeing', hypnosis, another reason for her being called 'Claire' comes to the surface. Furthermore, could the 'light', which her name also implies, perhaps refer to the supernatural light of the Nutcracker mentioned here, which is then received by her through mesmeric transfer? Regardless, the atmosphere becomes disturbed with rustling noises as midnight strikes.

The Clock strikes Midnight

'Midnight strikes. She [Claire] glances at the clock and sees in terror that the owl has been transformed into Drosselmayer, who looks at her with a mocking smile. She wants to flee, but her strength is lacking.' [130] And Drosselmayer, 'having spread out the flaps of his caftan, is waving them, exactly as an owl does his wings.' [131] At this point, it becomes obvious why

Vsevolojsky chose to change the colour of Drosselmayer's coat from the bright golden yellow in the Hoffmann and Dumas versions of the story, into a drab, earthen brown— owls in the natural world have wings of a browny hue; they are not golden yellow. As Drosselmayer waves the tails of his kaftan, it seems that he has now become the clock (not just its mender or maker), bringing to mind the words of de La Mettrie when he wrote 'the body is but a watch [a mechanical timepiece].' [132] Moreover, Drosselmayer has also become the owl; and an owl, 'keen-sighted at night, but almost blind by day [...] symbolised the seeker after 'vain knowledge', who could never see the truth.' [133] Certainly, in the guise of an owl, the bird of night that flies in the darkness, Drosselmayer is, metaphorically speaking, not about to set off in search of the light of truth. Furthermore, on a more sinister note, the owl is a symbol of ill omen and death. Is Drosselmayer then, as a flying owl, representing a dead soul, maybe *his own* dead soul which is departing life? This outcome is a possibility as Drosselmayer is not seen again by Claire after this sighting. [134] Perhaps Drosselmayer is intended to fly off, mounted on the clock? If so, the question arises: Does the notion of fleeing clock-time indicate a departure from the scientific world and earthly time? For the moment at least, Drosselmayer's disappearance from view heralds a realm of Claire's imagination, a dream world.

The Dream Symbolism of G H von Schubert

To ponder the meaningful essence of the 'dream' passages in *The Nutcracker* ballet, we must consider the highly relevant fact that, in the spring of 1814, Hoffmann asked the publisher of G H Schubert's *La Symbolique du Rêve* (*The Symbolism of Dreams*), Carl Friedrich Kunz de Bamberg, to send him a copy as quickly as possible.[135] This not only indicates Hoffmann's desire to read it, but, given that his own work, 'Nussknacker und Mausekőnig', was published just a couple of years later, and incorporated significant dream symbolism (in accordance with Schubert's tenets), it also shows that the influence of Schubert is hard to deny. Moreover, Vsevolojsky and Petipa, in their libretto of 1892, although they do not follow Hoffmann's dramatic detail to the letter, nevertheless maintain within it the influence of Schubert's dream concepts as relayed by Hoffmann.

Primary to Schubert's concepts of a dream state was the absence of reason. He writes that a dream state emerges gradually until 'finally, reason becomes dormant and the dreamlike universe hidden behind it appears in total freedom'.[136] For him, 'the voice of the conscience [in a dream], does not allow itself to be contested or snuffed out by any reasoning whatsoever, whether it be logical or grounded in common sense'.[137] In other words, there is no place for the scientific mind in a dream, and this situation remains true in the ballet, as Drosselmayer and the clock—symbols of the mind and mechanisms of the rational world—disappear from the stage at the point where Claire's reverie takes hold. The annotation in the piano reduction tells us: 'In the silence of the night, she [Claire] hears the scratching of mice. She wants to flee, but her fear is too great. She collapses into a chair. Everything disappears'.[138] And so it seems that Claire blacks out. In the apparent void left behind there now resides, if one follows Schubert's thinking, the universe of the dream, with its dream language which is akin to the original language of humans, 'the language of feeling and of love. [...] The words of this language which existed between God and man were the living organisms which still constitute today (but as shadows of the original) the nature which surrounds us.'[139] This very nature is a 'living dream,' a 'prophetic language' which was compared by Saint-Martin, the Unknown Philosopher, to a 'sleepwalker, speaking in a dream, who would act in all circumstances following the same inner compulsion, following the same unconscious and blind instinct, from which the actions of a sleepwalker arise.'[140] Moreover, it can be established from Schubert's description that such dream language is an unspoken language where words are images in nature, and actions are unconscious, like those of a somnambulist. This format of silent communication is obviously well suited to a ballet where no words are audibly spoken, and, in *The Nutcracker*, the role of the somnambulist who acts unconsciously is perfectly fulfilled by Claire herself. Indeed, for Schubert, the dream state where someone walks in their sleep is a superior state of mind, when one's capacity to love excels beyond space and time.[141] In this respect Schubert follows the trend of other thinkers of the period who viewed space as extension in human experience, and time as succession. Such notions were said to arise within the human mind, but not actually to exist in nature.[142] In the 'beyond', beyond space and time, there are therefore no clocks, and so the disappearance of the clock in the ballet is a necessity for the establishment of a genuine dream environment. Furthermore, in the absence of space and time, there are no barriers between the past, present and future; there are no barriers of distance. The sleepwalker can, under the influence of a magnetizer, even be transported effortlessly to another land which is totally foreign. And there, by means of long-distance clairvoyance, the future can be glimpsed. [143]

This early Romantic interest in dreams continued throughout the nineteenth century and was particularly evident in France at the *fin de siècle*. Victor Girard, writing during this time, stated:

> the maddest, strangest, most poetic and marvellous dreams have their origin within us. They are reminiscences, memories of life today and in the past; these dreams, blended with intuition, [...] form a fantastic melange. [...] The dream is an incomplete revelation of the mysteries of human destiny: it is the naïve, natural, sincere, spontaneous, direct and reflective expression of our thinking, of our intimate life. In cognitive man, on the other hand, reflection, will, reasoning, preoccupation with the moment, prejudices and imagination modify his ideas and his true individuality. [144]

In the ballet, the fantastic effect of such a dream world is immediately apparent when 'the Christmas tree [which has not disappeared] grows and becomes enormous.' [145]

The Christmas Tree grows

A note in Petipa's scenarios states: 'The back door opens and the Christmas tree becomes (apparently) enormous. 48 bars of fantastic music with a grandiose *crescendo*.' [146] And with the instruction of the door opening, the room, presumably,

becomes flooded with moonlight at ground level, as well as
at a higher level, thereby intensifying the moonlight already
shining through the window onto the Christmas tree with
its apples of glimmering gold and silver. The 'house of silver'
then truly comes into its own as the tree begins to ascend
upwards, magnificently, in wave-like musical surges punctuated with blasts from trumpets and the clashing of symbols.
The effect is wondrously magical and no doubt would
have pleased Tsar Alexander III and his son Nicholas, both
supporters of the ballet who had a penchant for the miracu-
lous. [147] But what does this awesome, grand transformation
of the tree achieve in stretching heavenwards? Claire does
not grow up with it. She is left at the foot of the tree among
the roots as if she has gone down! And worse than that, she
has (evidently) shrunk to the size of the toys and dolls that
have been left at the foot of the tree. Of course, all this is the-
atrically manipulated so that Claire's ensuing encounter with
the mice can be made visible in a credible way. But what can
this all mean? An explanation can again to be found in the
writings of Schubert.

The dream language of nature, as expounded by Schubert,
is a metaphorical language made manifest in dreams. He
states: 'Nature is the true basis of this metaphorical language
through which the divine has ever revealed itself.' [148] Its signi-
fication is like that of poetry, myth and ancient beliefs, which
use symbols from nature—like that of a tree—to elucidate
their meaning. [149] And so far, the Christmas tree in the ballet
has, as a metaphor, been linked with the Tree of Life, a symbol of rebirth. But now, at night, it paints a different picture
as it grows upwards. Indeed, it is documented in the *Zohar*

that 'at night-fall the Tree of Life soars up to heaven and its place is taken by the Tree of Death.'[150] Moreover, 'the *Zohar* regards it [the Tree of Death] as a symbol of the black arts which were one of the consequences of the Fall. It is linked to the existence of the psychic body deprived of the "body of light".'[151] By now taking the Christmas tree in the context of the Tree of Death, Claire's descent seems similar to a journey down into the underworld—and it must be said that the tree in mythology has long been seen as representing the three connecting levels of the cosmos: the topmost branches corresponding to the heavens; the trunk to the earth; and the roots to the underworld. And it is the roots of the Christmas tree that have become visible as it has grown.

The Dolls come to Life and the Hares sound the Alarm

The libretto continues: 'The dolls and toys come to life: the hares sound the alarm, the sentry in the sentry box raises his rifle and fires, the dolls run off in fright wringing their arms up in the air, seeking cover wherever they can.'[152]

The costume designs for what looks like a realm of childhood playthings are delightful. The dolls, of which three appear in the designs, are charmingly kitted out in dresses, bonnets and bows, arrayed in the French colours of red, white and blue. One even has a toy ram on a wheeled platform, reminiscent of the nursery rhyme character Bo-Peep. She is dressed in a white blouse and apron, a red skirt, and wears a yellow straw bonnet decorated with little red flowers.[153] This fancy aproned garb and straw hat is also reminiscent of the French queen, Marie Antoinette, who herself used to dress up as a shepherdess in a straw hat, pretending to take part in the simple, rural life of her hamlet farm with its farm animals at the *hameau de la reine* (the queen's hamlet) in the park of the palace of Versailles. [154] Given that the French monarchy was overthrown by the French revolutionaries and Marie Antoinette was guillotined in 1793, it is appropriate that this seemingly childlike caricature of her should be running away, arms aloft in distress at the gunshot from the military forces taking up position on stage.

The hares that sound the alarm (the word *lapin* (rabbit) is used in the French of Petipa's scenario) are pictured in the costume designs as grey hares/rabbits, with white fronts, pink ears and blue ribbons around their necks. In their hands are yellow drumsticks. [155] The hare or rabbit is a lunar animal which represents, amongst other attributes, intuition and 'light in darkness'. [156] Maybe that is why their drumsticks here are yellow, like sunlight. It is certainly going to be intuition that motivates Claire in this dream scenario as it unfolds.

The Mice do Battle with the Gingerbread Men
The libretto relates further: 'A detachment of gingerbread soldiers appear and line themselves into position. Hostile mouse troops begin the attack, drive back the gingerbread soldiers and, having won a complete victory, return with booty—pieces of gingerbread which they eat then and there'. [157]

The gingerbread men in the original costume designs are brown, just like the biscuits of today, but with white bits, perhaps sugar crumbs, coating the gingerbread. [158] They wear helmets and carry batons, bringing to mind Drosselmayer's harlequin dolls who also carried batons. Their appearance closely resembles Bertell's illustrations in the Dumas text of 1845. [159] The introduction of gingerbread men is apt for a Nuremberg location, as gingerbread is said to have been invented there in the Middle Ages. [160] Although the tradition of gingerbread baking remained particularly strong in Germany and Austria, it spread all over Europe, including Russia. [161] In the context of Napoleon and his alliance with Bavaria against Austria, the gingerbread men in the ballet can be equated with the inhabitants of the Tyrol (a mountainous area of Austria, lying to the south of Bavaria) who rebelled against the insurgent armies of French and Bavarian troops in 1809, but who were eventually quashed, just as the gingerbread men are. [162] And when the Nutcracker is described, in the Hoffmann and Dumas versions of the story, as wearing a 'little mountain dweller's hat', it could suggest that the Nutcracker is himself an alpine inhabitant, maybe a Tyrolean, of humble status. [163] But whatever the provenance of the Nutcracker, he *is* spurred on against the mice by the defeat of the gingerbread men.

The mice soldiers are more sinister. In the costume designs they are sketched in all-in-one, dark blue-grey suits, sporting a tail behind them. They have large pink ears and short cloaks tied around their shoulders, in a dark-blue velvety material, with a golden border and lighter-blue lining. They are of a wealthier appearance than the gingerbread men. They are also much more menacing, carrying long rods to which are attached sizeable serrated blades. In addition, their mean and lean pointed noses give them the appearance of rats as opposed to mice (in symbolic terms, however,

mice and rats are often indistinguishable). Mice are associated with death and destruction, as well as with avarice and
greed, and these attributes are borne out in the ballet when
the mice drive back the gingerbread men offstage, then return onstage, having presumably overcome them and sawn
them up into pieces with their serrated knives. The mice
even devour pieces of the gingerbread men's remains on the
stage. Superficially, it looks like a jolly fine feast, but more
seriously, the whole episode bears the hallmark of intrinsic
evil. And, indeed, the opposing presence of good and evil is
a primary image in Schubert's language of dreams.

The Conscience harbours Good and Evil in Dreams

Schubert, in his work *La Symbolique du Rêve*, stated that
the conscience was the instrument of the language of man
in days gone by, and that it *still* inspires the images in our
dreams. He writes: 'The conscience fully incorporates that
faculty of intuition [...] in which all the influences of a
spiritual world, superior or inferior, good or bad, take effect, and through which are expressed all the forces of a
past and future life'.[164] He admits that this dual presence of
the good and the bad is ambiguous, but it is always there
throughout man's life. He goes on to say that good or bad
spirits sometimes appear in a tangible form to the soul.
Surely, in *The Nutcracker*, the gingerbread men and the mice
can be reckoned as tangible forms of good and bad spirits of
conscience? Moreover, Schubert reiterates the absence of rational judgement in these dream circumstances, saying, 'no
mental reasoning [...] is capable of waylaying a soul that has
been touched by the contagious power of the Truth'.[165] In

other words, the content of the dream is totally uncluttered by earthly trappings: it is stark. And surely, too, the truth conveyed by the defeat of the gingerbread men could not be more stark than in the image of the mice physically devouring their remains. [166]

The Mice do Battle with the Tin Soldiers

At this juncture the Nutcracker (who like the other toys has come alive) jumps into action. The libretto continues: 'The Nutcracker, having witnessed the failure of the gingerbread troops, leaps up from his bed and orders the hares/rabbits to immediately sound the alarm again. The tops of boxes, in which were lying toy tin soldiers, fly open and from them marksmen, grenadiers, hussars and artillery men with copper cannon hastily crawl out'. [167] The tin soldiers are represented in the costume designs by the figure named 'Pantin' (puppet), and they look like tin men in plain, metallic coverings and pointed headgear. [168] They resemble armoured troops, trained to obey orders automatically; their forces are obviously going to be more effective than the gingerbread forces. They are referred to in the piano reduction as 'the old guard', and the Nutcracker shouts out to them the rallying call, 'Aux armes!' (To arms!). [169] At this point the Mouse King makes his entrance and is hailed by his troops.

The Mouse King

In the costume designs the character of the Mouse King is pictured as a large, tall rat-like mouse with body of dark-blue grey and pink ears, just like his mouse soldiers. [170] His clothes and accoutrements are, however, befitting his royal rank.

Noticeably, around his shoulders he wears a knee-length cloak of brilliant, vermilion red, bordered and patterned in gold; it is strung around his neck with a tasselled gold cord. Sewn on to the left side of his cloak is a star-shaped insignia which looks similar to Napoleon's Légion d'honneur (Legion of Honour), except that, instead of an eagle at its centre, another creature is featured sketchily, perhaps an owl. [171] On his head is a gold crown with five long spikes, a small dark-blue sphere adorning the tip of each spike. Maybe these spheres are meant to represent five continents in the underworld, corresponding to the five earthly continents? Around the Mouse King's neck is a necklace of dark-blue spherical beads. Necklaces, threading together separate entities, are a symbol of unity. In his right hand, he holds a long sceptred staff with a serrated blade at its lower end (just like the blades carried by his soldiers but larger and longer). He looks imperious and terrifying.

According to the libretto, 'The Mouse King orders his troops to resume the offensive. The mice attack a few times but stumble back with great losses: then the Mouse King enters into single combat with the Nutcracker. Claire, seeing the danger threatening her beloved, takes her bootee in her hand and, with all her strength, throws it at the Mouse King.' [172] Dumas, in his text, puts the matter more strongly: 'Marie [Claire] took off her shoe, and, with all her force, threw it into the middle of the mêlée, and she did this so adroitly that the terrible projectile hit the king of the mice so that he rolled into the dust.' [173] And then everything vanishes and Marie (Claire) faints. In the ballet, however, the Nutcracker goes on to take advantage of the situation. The

Nutcracker wounds his enemy (the Mouse King) who re-
treats with his entourage. [174] In either case, the effect of the
hit of Claire's shoe (whether bootee or slipper) seems to have
been crucial. But what does it signify?

The shoe, as a symbol of liberty, highlights Claire's newly
found freedom and courage to confront the Mouse King. [175]
But are her shoes just any old shoes? As mentioned earlier, in
the costume designs Claire's shoes/slippers are golden with
pointed toes. [176] If thrown with momentum, whirling through
the air, could they strike like a rotating Catherine wheel, like
a vehicle of piercing light that symbolizes the power to dispel
darkness and evil? Whatever its effect, Schubert, in analysing
the language of dreams, speaks of the actions of an individual as prophetically representing that of a whole nation and
its destiny. These destinies are 'always struggles of Truth ver-
sus Falsity, that of the ultimate and guaranteed victory of the
one over the other, and the perspective of a splendid kingdom of Light, of Love and of Ecstasy.' [177] Might Claire and the
Nutcracker, in this respect, represent their people in their
struggles against Napoleon? And might the defeat of the
Mouse King secretly refer to Napoleon's future downfall?

The drama of the ballet moves on apace. Claire faints
(as in the Dumas story), and when she comes round, the
Nutcracker 'has changed into a handsome prince; he kneels
before her and asks her to follow him.' [178] This is the moment
of the Nutcracker's declaration of love for Claire. As he
kneels before her it is almost (if not in fact) like a marriage
proposal. It is as if the trials and tribulations they have undergone—first, when Fritz broke the Nutcracker's jaw; and then,
when the Mouse King took up arms against them—have

transformed them and brought them together. This outcome aligns perfectly with Schubert's conclusion that 'the dream universe generally plays a major role in the development and flowering of the spirit.'[179] Moreover, for Schubert, as mentioned above, the language of the dream itself is the language of feeling and love, a love which demands a metamorphosis of the inner being and which often surfaces in significant and recurring dreams. It is a higher love, whose quest is the spiritual and divine.[180] He elaborates that:

> in a more frequent and surer way, this higher love is accustomed only progressively to take possession of a receptive soul and to fashion it after its own divine nature by imperceptible transitions. This method is the easiest and the gentlest, whilst the other, in which the mutations are more brutal and more sudden, is not devoid of violent struggle.[181]

In the ballet, it would seem that the love between Claire and the Nutcracker does move forward inwardly and progressively in peaceful stages: the brutal, sudden and violent circumstances are only outward. Furthermore, Schubert asserts:

> In as far as the somnambulist [Claire] participates in the knowledge and thought of the magnetizer [the Nutcracker], so the loving soul participates in this superior state, in the light of supreme Wisdom, in which are reflected, as in the universal source of all existence, the past, present and future, countries near and far. [...] As soon as love throws down the material mask behind

which it presently hides and starts to reveal itself in a
spiritual fashion, [...] it exercises [...] an attraction [...]
founded on its affinities which reach back to its origins.
That's why it is only in a state of somnambulism that
our capacity to love finds itself again in contact with
the realm above and receives from it a light in which
man seizes the sense, beyond space and time, of an
entire universe [...] although this capacity is not truly aware of its own existence other than through the
magnetizer himself. [182]

If one concedes to the Nutcracker the powers of a magnetizer to whom Claire has been drawn from the moment she
set eyes on him, then it appears quite natural that she would
follow him, even when the worldly reality of such an occur-
rence,—i.e., the elopement of a young man with a juvenile
girl, who leaves behind her parental home—is a circumstance never to be encouraged. The audience at this juncture
in the ballet, beguiled by the brave Nutcracker Prince, em-
pathizing with Claire, and transported by Tchaikovsky's
atmospheric music, must surely engage in a willing suspen-
sion of disbelief.

The libretto goes on: 'They [Claire and the Nutcracker]
go towards the Christmas tree and become hidden in its
branches.' [183] Presumably, in order to become hidden, the
pair must climb the tree to some extent, Claire following the
Nutcracker Prince, still entranced/magnetized by him. It is,
therefore, worth noting that in shamanism (a culture that
was still strong in Russian territories during the nineteenth
century, especially in Siberia) trees had mystical importance

and that 'climbing the tree or ladder [...] means the trip to
the other world, where the shaman gets into contact with
the gods, so that he could play the role of a mediator.' [184] In
this vein, the Nutcracker acquires the mantle of a shaman.
Moreover, this possible inference holds particular relevance
to Vsevolojsky himself, not just because *The Nutcracker* ballet he engineered with Petipa plays out finally in 'the other
world', but also because at the very beginning of his career,
after graduating from St Petersburg University, he worked
in the Russian interior ministry's 'Asia' department in St
Petersburg. [185] As a government official, he would certainly
have been aware of shamanism in the Asiatic lands of the
Russian Empire at that time. [186] And, more generally, there
was huge popular interest in native, pagan cultures (including shamanism) in Russia in the late nineteenth century. [187]
As the décor changes at this point, from a salon with a
Christmas tree into a whole forest of fir trees in winter, it is
difficult *not* to see the northern forests which sweep across
Russian Europe and Asia, and *not* to be reminded of the ancient, shamanistic beliefs which were once prevalent there.

Act I, Scene II

The Fir Forest in Winter

In Petipa's instructions by letter to Tchaikovsky, it is mentioned that, at the change of décor, 'Gnomes with torches are standing around the Christmas tree to pay homage to the prince, Clara [Claire] and the dolls, who are placed around the tree.'[1] Of course, it is common in folklore to find gnomes that inhabit forests: 'They came to symbolise the invisible being who, by inspiration, intuition, imagination or in dream, makes visible, things which are invisible. They exist within the human soul as flashes of knowledge, enlightenment or revelation. They are, as it were, the hidden soul of things.'[2] This idea that gnomes illuminate the mind is further emphasized here by the fact that they bear torches, for torches are themselves symbols of enlightenment. It was said that their 'light illuminated the passage of the Underworld and the paths of initiation.'[3] And so, as Claire and the Nutcracker proceed towards the thick of the Christmas tree, past the torch-bearing gnomes, it is as if they really are taking their leave of a dark underworld and embarking upon a winter's journey through a forest.

The libretto describes the setting as follows: 'The room changes into a dense forest of fir trees in winter. Snow begins to fall in large flakes and a storm brews.'[4] The set design for the forest by Mikhail Bocharov is a fine drawing of very tall mature pines, enclosing a central avenue cut through its middle.[5] It is not entirely dark, as the avenue affords some light. In travelling along this avenue, Claire and the Nutcracker continue the 'dream'. Appropriately, the collective symbol of a forest (as opposed to that of the individual tree) is known in dreams to represent the realm of the unconscious.[6] Indeed, the forest is a threshold symbol: there the soul enters the perils of the unknown; there it encounters the secrets of nature; and, for the shamans, it *is* the dwelling place of the spirits.[7] And the spirits of the forest in the ballet must surely be the snowflakes which are beginning to fall.

The Snowflakes

The snowflake depicted in the costume designs is a young girl with long, golden hair, in a knee-length tutu of white and pale gold, covered in blue-white balls (like balls of cotton) radiating out in rows from her dress.[8] She wears a white headband from which radiate sticks (probably made of wire), with more white balls, either in threes or fours, spaced out along their length. They construct a circular frame for her face. In her hand she holds a short, silver wand which branches out at the end, into a spray of five silvered 'twigs', each with two or three blue-white balls attached at equal intervals.

The libretto continues: 'The *corphées* and dancers of the *corps de ballet*, representing snow flakes, dance a *grand pas* (Waltz of the Snowflakes), finally forming into groups of picturesque snowdrifts. Gradually the storm dies away and the winter landscape brightens in the moonlight, which makes the snow sparkle like diamonds.'[9] The music for this dance is 407 bars long and lasts over six minutes.[10] The annotation on the piano reduction, notes at the start: 'The snow begins to fall. The whirlwind.'[11] Then at bar 257, with music growing very loud, a note in the orchestral score states: 'A strong gust of wind makes the snowflakes swirl.'[12] The timing changes to a very fast two beats in the bar, starting soft and then alternating between soft and loud, but gradually dying down. The whole effect is one of turbulence, no doubt assisted by the balls of white on the costumes bobbing and quivering and moving with the motions of the dancers. But why should this piece take so long when nothing very obvious happens in it? A newspaper review of 1892 reported: 'The second scene—a snowy forest—is not connected in any way with the story of the ballet and could also be omitted and interpolated into any other ballet.'[13] In other words, the piece is meaningless. Or is it? From a symbolic standpoint, 'whirlwinds were regarded as a manifestation of energy in nature, rising from a centre of power associated with gods, supernatural forces and entities who travel on whirlwinds or speak from them. The whirlwind thus becomes a vehicle for the divinity.'[14] On the other hand, perhaps the piece was simply inserted as a spectacle and made deliberately long in order that the audience could admire the novel effect of electrical light on the scene?[15] Maybe too, the length of the snow scene is meant to emphasize duration of time (which will be reinforced by the coming theatre interval at its close)—a duration which corresponds to the long, turbulent journey experienced by Claire and the Nutcracker as they fare through the forest?

The Journey in Dream Symbolism

The inspiration for the idea of a journey in the ballet may derive from Dumas' description of the journey of Drosselmayer's nephew, Christian Elias Drosselmayer, which lasted fourteen years and five months, taking him as far as the edge of a large forest bordering the foot of the Himalayas. [16] Certainly, Claire and the Nutcracker in the ballet have to have made their journey in a similar direction, even further in fact, as the opening scene of the final act finds them in a location with a distinctly oriental ring to it. But why make the journey at all?

Journeys undertaken by a hero or heroine are generally symbols of transformation. Whether the protagonists perilously cross a sea or travel through a forest fraught with danger, they are in search of something, a lost paradise, perfection, some truth etc.... The difference here is that Claire is making her journey in a dream, and therefore the conditions of that journey conform to the characteristics of dreams. Schubert remarks that:

> The somnambulist can also see himself transported [...] into a region where he has never been and which he only knows by name, where he sets eyes on what he has insistently been looking for and wanting. [...] These phenomena of long-distance clairvoyance [...] are equally caused by ecstasy, dreams, the unconscious, apparent death and other states devoid of any possibility of interaction with the exterior world. [17]

Indeed, Claire's journey with the Nutcracker would certainly appear, from this perspective, to be an internal journey of the mind, expressed outwardly by an environment of continuously gusting snowflakes. And the very physicality of being drenched in waves of large white snowflakes, as pure as the driven snow, symbolizes the inner experience of spiritual purification. Schubert, in *La Symbolique du Rêve*, indicates that the soul passes through a fair number of such purifications on its journey to the 'eternal homeland [i.e., heaven]'.[18] Therefore, taking account of Schubert's view, the perpetual onslaught of the windblown snow in the ballet would appear to accrue the significance of a series of purifying processes. Moreover, the prevalence in the choreography of circular shapes and turning movements, both on the spot and travelling, reinforce this idea of purification, as the circle itself is a sign of perfection.[19] And the snowflake balls themselves, as spheres—fluffy spheres of white which attach to the dancers' costumes—are also signs of perfection.[20] It is as if Claire and the Nutcracker are undergoing some sort of spiritual pilgrimage, an idea which is very much embedded in Russian culture. For in the Russian mind, spiritual pilgrimage is 'the impossibility of finding rest and peace in anything finite' and 'the striving towards infinity. [...] [It] is an eschatological striving which is waiting in the expectation that to everything finite there will come an end, that ultimate truths will be revealed'.[21] Such a hypothesis can explain the snow-swept progress of Claire and the Nutcracker, but, even more appropriate to this journey, are the dream concepts of shamanism which are native to Asiatic Russia.

In shamanism,

trance, sleeping and dreaming are states in which the
invisible world with its geography and inhabitants becomes available to the senses of living people. When
one is dreaming, [...] or falls into a trance, it is a sign
that some spirit or soul dimension has separated
from the person, even while another spirit may join
the person. Therefore all forms of non-waking conditions—unconsciousness, sleeping, dreaming, trance
[...] are associated with death and the separation of the
animating spirit from the body. They are all inherently
dangerous states, during which the person's soul wan-
ders about in the spirit world and from which it must
take care to return to the land of the living. [22]

It is interesting that this conception of the dream state
mentions that the shaman dreamer 'must take care to return to the land of the living.' In the ballet it is unresolved as
to whether Claire ever returns to her parental home. If she
has died, then the owl on the salon clock which flies off into
the night could be seen as a bird of death. The destination
of a shaman's dream, however, does not necessarily lead to
the kingdom of the dead, it can simply lead to another place
in the spirit world, for 'shamanism implies a worldview
that regards the universe and all its parts as interconnect-
ed and imbued with spirit forces that can interact with
human beings in positive or negative ways.' [23] Negotiating
these positive and negative spirit forces is, however, never easy for a shaman. [24] Nonetheless, the shaman's purpose
is to bring about balance between the positive and negative forces in the spirit world, even when this requires an

out-and-out battle. In adopting this standpoint, one can reflect retrospectively on the battle with the Mouse King as being a fight against a negative spirit. In shamanism, however, the fighting is but a balancing act, because if the negative/evil forces were killed, then nature would lose its balance. And in the ballet, the Mouse King is, in fact, not killed, just wounded. [25]

Overall, the dream itself is a manifestation of a shaman's ability to see spirits and navigate the invisible world. Spirits are connected to the three cosmic zones of air, earth and water and, as mentioned above, it *is* the duty of the shaman to bring balance and restore harmony between these spirits and humans. The shamanic dream pictures the continuing struggle for equilibrium—a state which involves some measure of intention and control by the dreamer. In the context of Claire herself as a shaman in the snow blizzard, it can be surmised that she *is* the calming, harmonizing force which brings the disturbed, flying snowflakes (water spirits in frozen form) to come to rest in a peaceful and orderly fashion at the end of the snowflakes' waltz. Such a conclusion would give Claire purpose in this snow scene, removing the idea that she is but a mere passive bystander to a picturesque, wintry change in the weather! Indeed, in shamanism, 'people and their environment are perceived as belonging to an ecological whole [...]. The creative transformation that is at the heart of shamanic [...] dream work is dependent on this view of the organic nature of being and beings. [...] As rain unfolds into the trees and trees into the wood [forest] [...] so the dream unfolds into reality.' [26] And it is this kind of 'reality', the 'reality' of Claire's dream 'where snow unfolds into the trees and trees into the wood,' which goes on to unfold into the 'reality' of the second and final act of the ballet which follows.

Act II

Confiturembourg

The setting for the second act of *The Nutcracker* is described in Petipa's scenario as 'The Magical Palace of Confiturembourg. A most fantastical décor.'[1] In the nineteenth century, the French word *confiture* referred to foodstuffs which had been boiled and then conserved in sugar, like sugared nuts and sweets, and fruits in syrup. The word *bourg* means 'town' and therefore 'Confiturembourg' can be deduced to be a manufacturing town of preserved sweetmeats.

Konstantin Ivanov produced two scenic backdrops for the final act of *The Nutcracker*.[2] Both are similarly oriental in appearance and have common features. For example, both scenes have a landing stage at the centre looking onto a small lake which stretches back to the bridged water entrance of a temple-like complex. The buildings of the complex are Indian-looking, architecturally, as are the side-gated areas that flank the central landing stage. The pillared gates of the landing stages and some of the temple-like buildings in the background are surmounted by stupas (hemispherical domes), indicating a Buddhist sanctuary.[3] However, there are significant differences. One difference is the trees that show up behind the side buildings and to the rear of the temple-like complex at the far side of the lake. In the backdrop which has a more Chinese aspect to it, there are tall Scots pines, smaller firs and even a miniature bonsai-looking pine in a pot under an arch. In the other backdrop, which has a more Tibetan or even Mongolian aspect to it, there are tall palms that grace the skyline behind the buildings. All these trees are noted for being symbols of life.[4] In the more Chinese-looking design, the sky is pink, and a broad orange banner, hung from the pinnacles of the side buildings, stretches across the stage, decorated with colourful swags from which are suspended what look like Chinese lanterns. In the more Tibetan/Mongolian-looking design, the sky is a deep turquoise-blue, and a broad brightly coloured stockade-type archway spans above the landing stage area, with a large bell-shape at its peak. This bell-shape could well represent a beehive, as below it, as well as above the archways of the side buildings, there are roundels which sport large winged insects, presumably bees—the bees which produce the honey for sweetening the preserves made in the town of Confiturembourg. Symbolically, the bee in Western culture is known to be an emblem of industriousness, as well as being emblematic of the soul and its materialization after death, and even of its resurrection. Moreover, 'in Greece, the beehive was often used as the shape of a tomb, suggesting immortality.'[5] In China, the bee is also representative of industriousness.[6] It may be that all these associations are implicit in the ballet, deliberately bringing together a mélange of East and West. In addition, the view of the bees in the roundels, looking down on their backs with wings folded into the body, corresponds to bee motifs displayed in trappings of the epoch of the Emperor Napoleon—such bee motifs show up prominently on the robes of the Emperor himself, embroidered in gold thread on a white satin ground.[7] For 'the bee had been incorporated into the imperial heraldry [...] to recall the bees found in the grave of Childeric I, the father of Clovis, the first Christian king of the Franks. Napoleon associated his reign with these early sovereigns of France.'[8] Clearly, Napoleon's choice of the bee stemmed from a desire for political legitimacy for his regime. And so it would appear that the significance of the bees for the audience can be taken in a number of contexts.

Both of Ivanov's stage landscapes give a gorgeously rich picture of an oriental paradise, reflecting a golden age. And indeed, the Romantics themselves 'looked beyond Greece toward Asia, toward the source of human wisdom, and exalted the childhood of mankind as imagined in India as the most original golden age, where a harmony of religion, philosophy and literature produced an existence for which the Romantic spirit yearned.'[9] For them, ancient India was a heavenly garden where nature and love were as one, and a pure innocence, like that of childhood, prevailed.[10] And so the glowing sets created by Ivanov, although fantasies, can, nevertheless, be viewed as perfectly mirroring this Romantic, nostalgic longing for an idyllic paradise past, an age of pure, golden innocence. And central to the concept of this pure innocence in the ballet is the presence of Claire, whose love for the Nutcracker *is* truly that of an innocent, young girl—a love which seamlessly blends as one into the surrounding environment.

Gotthilf Schubert, whose writings on dream states have already been examined in connection with the first part of the ballet, was, like other Romantics, also drawn to the East. For 'the influence of the unity of the wisdoms celebrated in the Romantic, mythical image of India is found most markedly in the natural philosopher Gotthilf Heinrich Schubert, [...] [especially] in his *Ansichten von der Nachseite der Naturwissenschaft* (1808), a work which profoundly influenced the writings of the later Romanticists, particularly E T A Hoffmann [...] He [Schubert] turns his glance towards the Orient, whence is to come the new happiness, the new redemption of mankind.' [11] Indeed, perhaps it should be Schubert's optimistic concept of the Orient as a recipe for the future, rather than as a nostalgic yearning for the past, that should be adopted when viewing Ivanov's stage settings. Certainly, they flag up the ultimate destination of the dream journey undertaken by Claire and the Nutcracker through the snowstorm in the forest.

Petipa's scenario states: 'The backdrop and wings portray gold and silver palm trees [an indication that the 'more Indian' Ivanov design was used]—sequins on the tulle [referring to stage hangings of fine net]. In the centre are fountains of lemonade, orangeade, almond milk and currant syrup. In the middle of these fountains, on the bank of a rosewater river, a pavilion of fruit drops with transparent columns can be seen.' [12]

The Sugar Plum Fairy

It is in the pavilion of fruit drops with the transparent columns that the sovereigns of Confiturembourg, the Sugar Plum Fairy and Prince Coqueluche, stand, awaiting the arrival of Claire and the Nutcracker Prince. They have prepared a reception for them and, on the rise of the curtain, duly move out from the pavilion accompanied by their reception party.

The original costume design for the Sugar Plum Fairy shows her in a full, white tutu to just above the knee, with bodice and strap-like sleeves on which is attached a short, stand-up gathered frill. [13] The whole costume is punctuated with deep pinkish-red plums of different sizes, the smaller ones on the bodice and sleeves, and the larger sizes on the skirt. The skirt is also flecked in gold. On the Fairy's head is a simple gold band, also decorated with small, deep pinkish-red plums which jut upwards like jewels. She holds a golden wand, tipped with a large, deep pinkish-red plum, crowned with a golden coronet. It appears that the Sugar Plum Fairy is nothing other than the Fairy who is responsible for the manufacture of sugared plums in Confiturembourg. However, in a more occult and oriental context, the colours of white and red are symbols of semen (equated with seed-essence and male life-force) and menstrual blood (the female 'essence'). [14] Adopting this imagery, the red plum seeds take on the appearance of drops of blood. In the more occult and Western context of alchemy, the colours of white and red are connected to the processes known as the 'albedo' (whitening of the philosopher's stone) and 'rubedo' (reddening of the philosopher's stone), but as the white here is almost certainly illustrative of the sugar of the sugared plums, it evokes more precisely the alchemist George Ripley's comparison of the perfected stone to sugar. [15]

As the esoteric symbolism of the Sugar Plum Fairy becomes more evident, one may suspect that it was this symbolism that initiated the choice of having a 'Sugar Plum Fairy' in the first place. For the character of the Sugar Plum Fairy and her consort do not appear in the original Hoffmann story of the 'Nussknacker und Mausekőnig', or in Dumas' version of it, and any interpretation has to solely rely on evidence from within the ballet itself. And here, in order to try and uncover the true faculties of the Sugar Plum Fairy, an examination of the costumed appearance of her suite (sketched by Alexander Vsevolojsky) may hold the clue.

The Suite of the Sugar Plum Fairy

The suite of the Sugar Plum Fairy (Suite de la Fée Dragée) is made up of eight fairies, named in the libretto as 'the fairies of melodies, flowers, images, fruits, dolls, nights, dancers and dreams.'[16] In the costume designs, all the fairies are given French names preceded by the designation 'Fée' (Fairy).[17] Clearly, the fairies are spirits of some kind, but what might they represent? The strongest evidence for their possible import emerges from the costume of the Fée des Beaux Rêves (Fairy of Good Dreams).[18] She wears a white tutu with black radiating rays edged with gold, and an overskirt of sky blue with gold stars. On the bodice front are two gold suns on her chest, with black radiating surrounds. On her head is a gold band, like a halo. She is veiled in a diaphanous blue veil with gold dots. She holds a golden staff topped with a golden sphere and surmounted by a gold crown. From this general impression, it can be surmised that her 'good dreams' are made in the heavens, but more significant is the image of the golden suns with black radiating surrounds. It depicts the moment when a golden sun fully eclipses a black sun so that only its black rays are visible. Following alchemical imagery, the black sun is the symbol of death; and the golden sun, in its obliteration of the black sun by eclipse, symbolizes resurrection and renewal of life. In a childlike, naïve way, one could correlate a bad dream to a black sun, and an eclipsing sun to the chaser-away of bad dreams. Credence is lent to this analysis in that another three fairies also bear alchemical elements in their imagery. One of these fairies is the Fée des Fruits (Fairy of Fruits). In her costume design, she is dressed in a pale sweet-pink tutu, with cherries patterning the hem. Small swathes of fruit adorn her shoulders, and fruit is wreathed around her waist. Her head is crowned with fruit, and she holds a staff with an apple at its upper end. [19] Alchemically, the fruits of trees (plums included!) symbolize the maturation of the opus (the so-called transmutation of base metals into gold), and golden apples in particular were used by alchemists to symbolize gold and the philosopher's stone. Another fairy, the Fée des Fleurs (Fairy of Flowers), bears similar traits. She is sketched in a white tutu-type dress with sash of bluebell blue. [20] Posies of flowers bedeck her shoulders, bodice and all along the hemline. She holds a staff with flowers at its top, and on her head sits a round basket, full of flowers. In alchemy, the flower is also a symbol of the opus: 'the beautiful colours which appear in the vessel at the fullest perfection of the work are represented as flowers blossoming from the plant of the stone'. [21] A fourth fairy, is the Fée des Bonnes Nuits (Fairy of Good Nights). She is drawn in a tutu of blue, with clouds around the hem. [22] Gold and silvered stars are above the clouds leading up to the waistline. The front of her bodice displays a gold star with silvered rays. Ostensibly, the idea of 'une bonne nuit' or 'good night' lies in the star-studded cloudless part of the sky, especially where the brightest of stars (as on the bodice) are bathed in silvered moonlight. Here, again, alchemical connotations can be drawn, for a mélange of silvered moonlight and golden starlight indicate the presence of Luna (the moon) and Sol (the sun). 'Psychologically, Luna governs the realm of the imagination [including the dream]. The white work of the albedo [the whitening/silvering process in alchemy] involves the cleansing of the subconscious [...]. When this is accomplished, the purified soul may become illumined.'[23] Following this prescription, the picturesque vignette on the tutu of clouds clearing to reveal golden stars in silvered moonlight signifies a purification of the soul's unconscious, which enables it to become illumined. Already in the ballet, the audience have witnessed such an event, when clouds cleared, falling as moonlit glistening snow onto Claire and the Nutcracker Prince in the forest, making them ready—ripe like fruit, one could say, or open like flowers in bloom—to become illumined by the sun. Of course, all this alchemical imagery has to be the gloss of Alexander Vsevolojsky himself as illustrator, and as it harks back to Western imagery, it appears to be incongruous with the oriental setting in which it is located. However, this interjection of alchemical content seems unlikely to have been arbitrary on the part of Vsevolojsky who was well educated and knowledgeable. Alchemical ideas were, besides, already well established in China by the beginning of the Christian era.[24]

The remaining four fairies in the suite of the Sugar Plum Fairy do not particularly appear to reflect alchemical imagery in their costume designs. They seem much more mundane, so to speak. The first of these is called the Fée Mélodie (Fairy of Melodies). She wears a tutu of light blue and wings to match.[25] A gold musical stave adorns her skirt surround, and the skirt is dotted all over with gold dots. On her bodice are displayed two harps, and she carries a gold wand which may represent a conductor's baton. Her powers are evidently connected to music and its orchestration. The presence of the harp, however, evokes the symbolism of the ladder which leads to the next world. The fact that there are two harps would therefore suggest two worlds, heaven and earth, one harp or ladder leading up to heaven and the other back to earth, a dual destination if you like. A second fairy is called the Fée Poupée (Fairy of Dolls). Her tutu is orange, with dolls in a patterned row decorating the hemline.[26] There are two dolls' faces on her bodice, and the staff which she holds has a doll's head at the top. This fairy's function appears to be a maker of dolls. A third fairy is called Fée Pantin (Fairy of Puppets). She is clothed in a tutu panelled in peach and white, the white panels being striped with horizontal gold stripes.[27] Gold pom-poms go round the hem, the shoulders, the sides of the panels and around her neck. She holds a stringed puppet, making it obvious that she is a puppeteer. The fourth remaining fairy is called Fée des Images (Fairy of Images). Her skirt is slightly longer than that of the others, reaching to below the knee.[28] Around the hem are scenes from life in panels, including a horseback rider. A red overskirt is ruched up like a theatrical curtain with gold-braided tasselled cord. Her bodice is patterned into squares of diverse colours. On her head is a hat which is made in the form of an artist's palette with two paintbrushes. This fairy is a scene painter, as in a theatre. And indeed, the four fairies as a group bear the characteristics of a puppet theatre production team: the first, the Fairy of Melodies, as musical director; the second, the Fairy of Dolls, as dollmaker; the third, the Fairy of Puppets, as puppeteer; and the fourth, the Fairy of Images, as scene painter. Their features effuse a childlike enchantment about them, in keeping with a children's story. But might their very nursery-like innocence not be a cover for something more serious? The visual references to a theatre and its staging conjure up the analogy of the world itself as being a stage, and the famous quotation from Shakespeare is brought to mind, 'All the world's a stage, and all the men and women merely players.'[29] Moreover, if these four fairies refer to the world and its tangible composition, and the other four fairies refer to the more heavenly, spiritual values of resurrection and illumination (albeit expressed alchemically), then the suite of the Sugar Plum Fairy would appear to be constituted of capacities equally distributed between earth and heaven, between the physical and the metaphysical. Admittedly, it would be difficult for an audience to read such detail into the characters of these fairies, especially if one were viewing the performance at some distance from the stage. Nevertheless, the import of the costume designs for the Sugar Plum Fairy's suite provide a useful clue as to the powers invested in the Sugar Plum Fairy herself, and as to how they might relate to the business of Confiturembourg.

Although there is no exact parallel in the Dumas text for the Sugar Plum Fairy and her suite, there is, however, an unseen phenomenon named as 'confiseur' (implying a 'confectioner' or 'maker of confections'), whom the inhabitants revere. The Sugar Plum Fairy herself, as revered sovereign of Confiturembourg who gives the orders, corresponds most closely to this persona of 'confiseur'. Moreover, in the Dumas text, the Nutcracker Prince explains to Marie (Claire) that the people of Confiturembourg are 'under the superior influence of a principle called *confiseur* which, at its pleasure, renders to them their form, having undergone a more or less prolonged process of cooking/baking'.[30] This description of Confiturembourg's people as being products of cooking/baking helps to explain the physical presence of the sweetmeats in the ballet who follow the Sugar Plum Fairy and her suite.

The Sweetmeats

On stage at the beginning of the final act are nine different sweetmeat personages. They are listed in the libretto as 'caramel, barley sugar, chocolate, petits fours, nougat, mint pastilles, *dragées* [sugared fruits], pistachios and almond snaps, picturesquely grouped, [who] bow before her [the Sugar Plum Fairy]'.[31] In the costume designs, all these personages are charmingly sketched with the addition of 'Galette' and 'Brioche'.[32]

The sweetmeat penned 'Caramelle' is dressed in a white dress and hat, and wrist ruffs all fringed with curling white tendril-like ends, similar to those paper accoutrements found on food in order that the eater can pick them up without getting sticky fingers![33] The only real indicator that Caramelle actually represents caramel is a blue sash slung over her right shoulder diagonally and tied at her waist, which has 'CARRAMEL' (*sic*) emblazoned on it in gold lettering. Her

tights and slippers are bright red. The sweetmeat penned
'Galette' wears a round flat hat in the shape of a flat, gold-
en cake—which is what a *gallette* is. [34] Moreover, the hat is
marked into wedges, in similar fashion to her skirt which
splays out in wedged panels over an underskirt of white. Her
sleeves are also made like round *gallettes*, with holes in their
centre for her arms; and her bodice is comprised of wedges crossed over in front. All parts of the 'cake' are marked
over with a criss-cross pattern. In her right hand, Gallette
holds a sharp, wedged cake knife, which would not only have
cut the cake, but would also have imprinted the criss-cross
patterning. The sweetmeat penned 'Dragées' appears in a
bright, deep pinkish-red puffball skirt which bulges out at
the waist and is drawn in to just below the knee. [35] The word
'DRAGÉES' is emblazoned around the front of the skirt in
bold gold lettering. The skirt is drawn in at the waist with
a thick golden cord, tasselled at its extremities. Her bodice is white, adorned with what look like white and deep
pinkish-red plums. Her sleeves are concocted of more of
these red and white plums, as is her headdress which holds
one large red plum on the crown of her head, surrounded by three smaller white plums. Clearly the white colour
represents sugar coating for the plums. This sweetmeat
stands out from the rest as representing a particular product relating to the Sugar Plum Fairy herself. The sweetmeat
penned 'Brioche' (Sweet Bun) is sketched in a brown dress,
with flared skirt to below the knee. [36] There is a bustle on
the back of the skirt looking like a lump of dough or cooked
bun, two small round buns stuck on the shoulders in lieu of
epaulettes, and a roll of dough on her brown bonnet which

curiously mimics the Phrygian cap shape seen earlier in the costume of Marianne. Over her dress she wears a blue and white striped apron, and a blue neckscarf tied in a bow at the front. [37] The sweetmeat penned 'Petits Fours' is depicted in a very wide, round, white tutu which is decorated with three tiers of brightly coloured shapes—almond shapes at the top, lozenges in the middle and circular shapes at the foot. [38] They presumably represent different types of petits fours. The hemline of the skirt is serrated, with round balls (probably fruit drops) hanging down from the teeth of the jagged edging. On her head is a broad-brimmed white hat which projects upwards in tubular fashion like a round box, or even like a baking tin which is serrated at the top edge. Sweets crowd round the upper surface of the broad brim, and risen pastry appears to protrude from the open crown of the hat. In her hands she holds a cornucopia gilded in gold and silver. The cornucopia is a symbol of endless bounty and of fertility, and it is appropriately filled here with a profusion of sweets. The sweetmeat penned 'Nougat' is shown in a very pale-pink tutu patterned with different coloured, nut-like ingredients. [39] She also wears a white hat like a crown, with a wide brim laden with sweets. The sweetmeat penned 'Pastille de Menthe' (Mint Pastille) wears a tutu of silvery white with white balls (presumably representing mint pas-tilles themselves). [40] A feathery sea-green string, presumably the stem of a mint plant, is strung over her shoulders. The sweetmeat penned 'Sucre d'Orge' (Barley Sugar) is clothed in a white tutu with golden dots, presumably represent-ing barley sugar drops, and with spiral stripes in gold and plum. [41] Her headdress consists of plum-looking sweets.

She holds a stick, like a candy stick, spirally striped in gold and plum. The sweetmeat penned 'Praline' wears a dark, chocolate-brown tutu with puffed sleeves, presumably representing the chocolate coating which is used to surround a praline sweet filling.[42] The skirt has pom-poms around the hem and around the dropped waist, perhaps representing round chocolate pralines themselves. She carries a long stick with a round placard at the top stating 'PRALINES'. The sweetmeat penned 'Pistache' (Pistachio) is sketched wearing a light-cream tutu, the overskirt of which is like a bursting nut.[43] The underskirt is pistachio green. Her headdress of cream and pistachio green portrays half a nut, presumably a pistachio nut, which sits on her head. The nut is, of course, a seed which initiates reproduction, complementing the fertility symbol of the cornucopia held by Petits Fours. But symbolism of a seed 'rises above the cycle of plant reproduction to acquire the meaning of the alternation of life and death'.[44] Certainly, the idea of regeneration is mentioned in Hoffmann's 'Nussknacker und Mausekönig', and in the Dumas version when the Nutcracker Prince explains to Claire that, 'the people of Confiturembourg believe, through their own experience, in metempsychosis'.[45] Moreover, the image of the outer casing of a nut cracking or bursting open to free the kernel inside, in a process of regeneration, casts light on what the function of a 'Nutcracker' prince in this ballet might be. In the physical context of Confiturembourg, it would now seem that the function of the Nutcracker Prince is related to the liberation of nuts/seeds from their shells in order for them to be made into various confections. And the liberty cap that the prince wears, in the design of

the wooden nutcracker given by Drosselmayer, would therefore now appear to relate to that same freeing of the nuts.
The sweetmeat penned 'Macarons' (Macaroons) appears
in a plum-red tutu and a white apron bib, with white apron
panels as an overskirt, and six macaroon cakes on each panel
aligned in a downward row. [46] Half a nut is placed as a hat
on her head. This nut is likely to be an almond or coconut
which were common ingredients for this sweet light biscuit.
The principal colours of her white and red ensemble can be
associated with the Sugar Plum Fairy's costume, suggesting
some culinary link.

The import of the costumes of the sweets is difficult to de-
termine per se, especially as there is no dancing role attached
to them. Perhaps they are simply the regenerated materialization of dead souls as symbolized by the bees. Reviewers of the
time were critical of the fact that there seemed to be neither
rhyme nor reason for the extravagance bestowed upon them.

> The third scene represents the 'Kingdom of the Sweets'
> in the original decoration of Mr Ivanov, consisting of
> such an abundance of fruit drops, confections, and
> gingerbreads that just looking at it is cloying. Strictly
> speaking, there is no ballet in this scene, but only an
> exhibition of costumes which flaunt luxury and their
> more or less remote likeness to caramels, sugarplums,
> mint cakes, and other products. [47]

Indeed, the meaning of these sweetmeats' costumes is enigmatic. And because there is no dancing which merits their
presence, the sweets (as well as the non-dancing suite of

the Sugar Plum Fairy) are cut from modern productions. However, a clue as to a *raison d'être* for the sweetmeats could be construed from the 'small silver soldiers who guard the palace' and who accompany them on stage.[48]

The Reception Party—the Silver Soldiers, Moors, Pages and Major-Domo

The costume designs for the silver soldiers (marked as twelve in number and described as 'Soldats d'argent') reveal silver-armoured knights wearing helmets topped with ragged-looking wings, and holding long poles, bearing silvery moths at the upper ends, again with ragged wings as if they had been eaten into.[49] The key to their function would appear to lie in the motif of the moth. For the moth, sometimes called the 'night butterfly', 'is the constant symbol of the soul seeking the Godhead and consumed by a mystical love, attracted like the insect fluttering round the candle until it burns its wings.'[50] Perhaps the raggedness of the moths' wings on the soldiers' poles relates here to souls who have somehow flown too close to the 'light' and died. So the question arises—Do these soldiers of silver guard souls of the dead? And if they do, what is the destiny of these souls? Moreover, if the town of Confiturembourg follows Buddhist precepts, as has been supposed from Ivanov's staged architecture, then there are two outcomes for souls which have departed from the world: they can either attain Nirvana (a state of bliss, free from rebirth); or they can be reborn back into the world in any form. In Buddhism, if the soul is reborn, then it undergoes an intermediate existence, transitional between lives on earth. Conversely, for those destined

1. Costume design for Claire, in *The Nutcracker*, Act I, Scene I.

2. Illustration of the Silberhaus family, in *Histoire d'un casse-noisette*.

3. Costume design for Drosselmayer, in *The Nutcracker*, Act I, Scene I.

4. Illustration of Drosselmayer, in *Histoire d'un casse-noisette*.

5. Illustration of Fritz, in *Histoire d'un casse-noisette.*

6. Costume design for the Sutler, in *The Nutcracker*, Act I, Scene I.

7. Illustration of the Nutcracker doll, in *Histoire d'un casse-noisette.*

8. Costume design for the Nutcracker doll, in *The Nutcracker*, Act I, Scene I.

9. Illustration of the owl clock, in *Histoire d'un casse-noisette.*

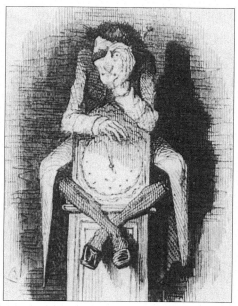

10. Illustration of Drosselmayer on the owl clock, in *Histoire d'un casse-noisette.*

11. Illustration of the gingerbread men, in *Histoire d'un casse-noisette.*

12. Illustration of the mice eating the gingerbread men, in *Histoire d'un casse-noisette.*

13. Costume design for the Mouse King, in *The Nutcracker*, Act I, Scene II.

14. Illustration of Claire throwing her slipper, in *Histoire d'un
casse-noisette*.

15. Costume design for a snowflake, in *The Nutcracker*, Act I, Scene II.

16. Costume design for the sweetmeat, Brioche, in *The Nutcracker*, Act II.

17. Costume design for a flute player, in *The Nutcracker*, Act II.

18. Costume design for a golden flower, in *The Nutcracker*, Act II.

19. Illustration of Claire and the Nutcracker on the rosewater river, in *Histoire d'un casse-noisette*.

20. Costume design for the Sugar Plum Fairy, in *The Nutcracker*, Act II.

21. Costume design for Prince Coqueluche, in *The Nutcracker*, Act II.

22. Photo of Vavara Nikitina as the Sugar Plum Fairy, and Pavel Gerdt as Prince Coqueluche.

23. Stage design for the salon, Act I.

24. Author's sketched detail of a moth from the design for the silver
soldiers.

for Nirvana, they merely experience a passing point on
their journey which never returns to earth. In either event,
Confiturembourg would seem to take on the role of some
kind of transmigratory staging post for the soul. The suite of
the Sugar Plum Fairy, as mentioned above, appear as spirit
agents, equally capacitated in actions leading towards either
earthly or heavenly destinations. Might their real purpose be
to facilitate a soul's onward journey, wherever that may lead?
On the other hand, the outward impression of the cohort of
sweetmeats, which shouts only of abundance, variety, rich-
ness and materiality, suggests an earthbound destination.
Might the sweetmeats be personifications of souls undergoing an intermediate existence before being re-born on earth?
     Petipa's scenario continues:

     The Major-Domo [master of ceremonies], having
     spied the approach of his expected guests, positions
     little Moors, and pages whose heads are of pearl, bod-
     ies of rubies and emeralds, and legs of pure gold; they
     carry oil burners. Claire and the Nutcracker quietly sail
     along the river in their gilded nutshell.[51] On their dis-
     embarkation onto the embankment, the silver soldiers
     salute, and the Moors, in costumes made from the iri-
     descent feathers of a hummingbird, take Claire by the
     arm and carefully help her onto dry land.[52]

The little Moors mentioned here are the first to receive
Claire in Confiturembourg. The costume designs paint
them in royal blue and gold suits, holding yellow parasols
fringed with small, gold hanging bells.[53] The royal blue and

gold brushstrokes of their suits would seem to prescribe the richly blue feathers of a hummingbird catching the light of the sun. The parasol, its roundness being associated with the sun, is a solar symbol, appropriately coloured yellow here. It is also a symbol of 'power, both temporal and spiritual', and thereby adds to the duality contained in the idea of Confiturembourg's location as being somewhere between heaven and earth. [54] But why include the feathers of a hummingbird, a bird which is not a native of the Far East today? [55] The simple answer would appear to reside in the hummingbird's appetite for nectar, which it extracts from flowers. Nectar, or honey, is, in Western culture, the food of the gods, the food of immortality. [56] In Eastern culture, honey 'came to denote the peak of spiritual bliss and the state of Nirvana'. [57] The little Moors (as hummingbirds) therefore not only signal the proximity of nectar, but also, symbolically, the proximity of eternal spiritual blessedness. Moreover, clad in the iridescent feathered plumage of a bird, they don the symbol of a winged soul ready for illuminated transcendence. [58] So the little Moors who welcome Claire and assist her on her arrival can be deduced as ascending dead souls. And Claire herself, in these circumstances, can now surely be considered as a dead soul too. Moreover, the little Moors' immediate taking of her into their fold also insinuates that she is, like them, destined for illumination and for Nirvana, and will not be re-born on earth. Certainly, in the ballet, Claire never exits from her dreams to find herself back in her bedroom, as she does in the Hoffmann story.

The pages, who are lined up alongside the little Moors, are made out of gold and jewels (pearls, emeralds and rubies), and also harbour symbolic meaning. For, in Buddhism, jewels are symbols of wisdom, that most treasured of treasures. [59] Clearly, these pages are no ordinary pages, each page holding a golden burner of fragrant oil, and (as shown in the costume designs) a lotus flower. [60] The white lotus flower is considered to be the '"Flower of Light", the result of the interaction of the great creative forces of the fire of the sun and the lunar powers of the water'. [61] (And in this respect, remember the name 'Claire' itself means 'light'.) Furthermore, 'the lotus depicts spiritual unfolding as it starts with its roots in the slime and, growing upwards through the opaque waters, it flowers in the sun and the light of heaven'. [62] Claire's journey has similarly progressed, starting by the dark roots of a tree during a winter's evening, and arriving in a land of bright, summer sunlight. In addition, the lotus depicts death and rebirth in Graeco-Roman art, whilst in Buddhism the lotus depicts wisdom and Nirvana. If Confiturembourg *is* an interim location, either prior to going back to earth, or on to Nirvana, then the lotus can be a sign for both destinations. Thus, Vsevolojsky seems to have woven a fusion of the symbolism of East and West into his original ballet designs.

Last, but not least to receive Claire and the Nutcracker Prince on the landing stage, is the Major-Domo (master of ceremonies). He is given the title in the original costume designs 'Petit homme de brocarte d'or' (Little man in gold brocade), and he is magnificently clothed in gold and white, wearing a cavalier-styled hat of gold, with a long, swirling white plume. [63] Here, the colours of gold and white on his garments echo the white dress with gold sash worn by Claire in the first act.

As the couple set foot on dry land, they alight onto a carpet spread out by the little Moors which is sprinkled with mint lozenges and angelica flowers. [64] Appropriately, angelica is a herb which grows in the Far East; its stem and petals are used in confectionery and it is therefore well suited to this town of confectioners. Traditionally, because of its healing herbal properties, it has also been used as an amulet. [65] And it may be, partly at least, as an amulet that these flowers have found their place here. Etymologically, angelica's European name refers to angels, and qualities of purity and perfection which one can readily assign to Claire. On the other hand, angelica's Chinese name literally means 'return', which one can just as readily assign to the Nutcracker Prince, who is indeed returning to his family. [66]

Claire and the Nutcracker arrive in Confiturembourg

As Claire and her prince step ashore, they are re-costumed, not in an Eastern style as one might deem appropriate, but curiously, still in Napoleonic fashion. The costume design for Claire, marked 'Claire en Merveilleuse', shows her attired in a white high-waisted gown decorated all over with tiny gold *fleurettes* and ruched up with branches of laurel. [67] A trailing sash around her waist and shoulder is of pale pink and there is a pale-blue beading on the shoulder. On her head sits a turban of white, pink and green. At its front, in the centre, shines a large blue stone from which are secured three large peacock feathers which boldly flare upwards, like flames. As mentioned previously, the laurel branches, as Napoleonic decoration, are indicative of victory. However, the laurel, as an evergreen, also signifies eternity and immortality. This latter symbolism is also attributed to the peacock and its feathers, evidence of which can be found in both Eastern and Western cultures. As for the blue stone, perhaps a sapphire, its blue colour symbolizes truth; and here, fastened on her brow, the sapphire more specifically suggests the *contemplation* of truth. [68] As for the stylized golden *fleurettes*, they, like the laurels, were a frequent decoration on clothing and artefacts belonging to the nouveaux riches of Napoleon's France. [69] 'Under the Consulate and the Empire, flowers [...] served to magnify the riches of France, which were able to flourish thanks to political and military success.'[70] Here in this oriental setting, they could also signify the yellow lotus (implying immortality) or even the 'golden flower' of Buddhism and Taoism (denoting spiritual rebirth). [71]

The costume design for the Nutcracker, marked 'Casse-Noisette en Incroyable', depicts him donned in long, white, fitted trousers and white stockings with a pink horizontal stripe. [72] His waistcoat is also white, edged in a banding of pink and green-blue, and worn under a pink tailcoat with a dark pink stripe. On his head is a white wig *en incroyable*, and in his hand he holds a black bicorn hat typical of high-ranking military personnel during the Napoleonic period. On his chest, a deep-red ruby is centrally attached to his shirt. The bright colours of pink, white and blue are reminiscent of the vivid hues of the Orient and also of the different shades of lotus blooms. As the style is not oriental, however, and the black bicorn hat reminds one of paintings of the Emperor Napoleon (bringing to mind, in particular, those portraying him surveying the battlefield at the scenes

of his famous victories, looking over, inescapably, the car-
nage of conflict), might the Nutcracker's black bicorn hat
symbolize death? But, if the black hat symbolizes death, we
must also pay heed to the majority of the Nutcracker's costume being white, and symbolic perhaps of life and the role
of a nutcracker as something that engineers the liberation
of seeds and nuts from their shells to regenerate. The fact
that the black hat is not on the Nutcracker's head at this
time may suggest that dark thoughts, such as death, are far
from his mind—indeed, the white wig, which *is* on his head,
could signal the opposite, i.e., thoughts of light. When one
factors in the ruby-red stone worn on his chest—a symbol
of passion and love—then the Nutcracker begins to look
like a bridegroom, and Claire, in her long white gown, is
perfect for a bride. [73]

At the moment of arrival, the libretto states:

> From the rays of a scorching sun, the sugar kiosk on the
> rose river slowly begins to melt and finally disappears;
> the fountains cease flowing. The Sugar Plum Fairy with
> Prince Coqueluche and the princesses—sisters of the
> Nutcracker—greet the new arrivals as the Fairy's suite
> bows reverentially and the Major-Domo welcomes the
> Nutcracker Prince on his safe return to the castle of
> Confiturembourg. [74]

In the reception party, the four princesses who are the
Nutcracker's sisters, do not, like many of the participants in this final opening scene, have a dancing role and
their presence is minimal. However, two designs for their

costumes survive. Both portray young ladies in long gowns like Claire's, wearing coronets of blue velvet. [75] In the first sketch, their gowns are of pale yellow and pale blue; in the second sketch, their gowns are white with a high collar, and long blue train, all of which is decorated with gold *fleurettes*. Stylistically, it would seem the sisters are of European origin, clothed in colours commonly associated with the blue of the sky, symbolic of truth; with the gold of the sun and the stars, symbolic of spiritual illumination; and the white of light, symbolic of purification. [76] But the location of the princesses in the Far East invites a complementary gloss, for, in Buddhism, blue is the colour of wisdom; gold the colour of light; and white the colour of spiritual transformation. [77] Moreover, 'in India, and in Indo-Tibetan Buddhism [...] experience of the light signifies a meeting with ultimate reality' and 'in China, experience of the light also denotes passing beyond worldly consciousness'. [78] Although actual particulars of the four princess sisters are not given in the libretto, the general visual impression is one of heavenly maidens (akin to Western representations of the Virgin Mary) who have arrived to greet their brother.

Petipa's scenario describes the encounter as follows:

Behind them [the pages], follow four doll-like ladies, so splendidly and richly dressed that Claire recognizes them unmistakably as royal princesses of Confiturembourg. All four, on seeing the Nutcracker, embrace him simultaneously with heartfelt affection, exclaiming together: 'Oh, my prince! Oh my dear prince! Oh, my brother! Oh, my dear brother!'

The Nutcracker, very deeply moved, having taken Claire by the arm, turns excitedly to the princesses: 'My dear sisters, this is Mlle. Claire Silberhaus, whom I present to you, it is she who has saved my life. For, if she had not thrown her shoe at the Mouse King at that very moment when I was losing the fight, then I would now be lying in a grave, or, even worse, would be devoured by the Mouse King.'

'Oh, dear Mlle. Silberhaus, oh, noble rescuer of our dear and beloved prince and brother' [they replied]. [79]

This whole encounter is very touching and perfectly appropriate for the occasion. However, the word 'rescuer' here in Russian is 'спасительница', which in religious terms denotes 'saviour'. [80] The word used in the French scenario is 'libératrice', which not only means a liberator, but can also be construed as a 'redeemer' or 'saviour'. [81] But why should Claire, who, on the face of it, merely forced the Mouse King into retreat by throwing her shoe at him, merit this more elevated status of 'saviour'? An answer could be in the ideas of salvation and liberation which constitute Nirvana in Buddhism, ideas which relate to the state of heavenly bliss which a soul arrives at having been liberated or saved from the earthly cycle of birth and rebirth. However, in order to be 'saved' or 'liberated', the soul, as referred to above, *has* to see the 'light'. When Claire (whose name means 'light') threw her golden slipper/shoe at the Mouse King, the Nutcracker, metaphorically speaking, 'saw the light', and was therefore 'saved', foregoing a physical death in a grave, and, in Buddhist terms, liberated thereafter. A critic of the day caught the dilemma of the libretto when he reported: 'The librettist apparently was not able to take full advantage of the subject matter or, perhaps, this story is too fantastic and complicated for pantomime.'[82] This latter comment about the libretto being 'too fantastic and complicated' highlights its difficulties of interpretation for an audience. Perhaps the fantastic and complicated libretto attracted the occult mystical interests of the imperial Russian family at the time of the ballet?[83] It certainly alluded to knowledge of the cultures of the East, which Russians then were bringing back to St Petersburg through the exploration and acquisition of lands.[84] But whatever the hidden agenda, all this sumptuous ceremony has not survived in modern productions to any great extent, and not least because the *raison d'être* behind it remains obscure.

The reception is finally brought to a conclusion when, 'as if by magic at a signal from the Sugar Plum Fairy, a table appears on stage, resplendent with preserved fruits etc. [...] and the short gentleman [Major-Domo] orders chocolate to be served.'[85] An entertainment follows.

The *Divertissements* of Chocolate, Coffee and Tea

The Spanish Dance

The entertainment commences with *divertissements* designated as 'Chocolate', 'Coffee' and 'Tea'.[86] Ostensibly, they represent dances from Spain, Yemen and China, and are danced not by lumps of chocolate, coffee grains or tea leaves, but by people dressed in costumes from these countries. Unlike the sweetmeats, who are personifications of edible confectionery, the dancers of the Chocolate, Coffee and Tea dances are worldly people who, because they are here located in Confiturembourg, can be deemed to be purveyors to Confiturembourg of the products which give their names to their dances. And because Spain, Yemen and China are linked by sea routes, from West to East, it would seem that their choice is a logistical one, as well as a choreographic one on account of the flavour which the national dances of these countries contribute to the *divertissements* themselves. [87]

Tchaikovsky's music for the Spanish dance, 'Chocolate', is a very lively piece, *allegro brillante* in 3/4 time. It opens with a trumpeting bravura for couples of men and women. The vivacity of the dance is matched by the bright colours of their costumes, in traditional hues of red and yellow, black and white. [88] There are four original designs: two for women, and two for men. In one of them, a lady in a plush Spanish dress of plum-pink and white holds a black fan in one hand and, in the other, a plate with cup and saucer on it, a spoon protruding from the cup. The cup and saucer allude to chocolate as a 'drink', which is how it was mainly considered in Spain since the discovery of the cocoa plant (from which it was made) in the Spanish Americas in the sixteenth century. At the time of the ballet's premiere, chocolate was still the favoured drink of the Spaniards. In another of the designs, a man is dressed in pale-yellow breeches and waistcoat, a white shirt and a black bicorn-like hat. The military aspect of the bicorn-looking hat reminds us of the years 1808-1813 when Napoleon's brother Joseph was the Spanish king, and which is also the period that the ballet is set in. [89] Furthermore, the hat is unusually decorated with medallions on the middle and back peaks which surround dark, roundish centres. Within the context of chocolate, these 'dark, roundish centres' can be perceived as representations of roasted cocoa beans. In addition, the Spaniard clasps a castanet in his left hand, clacking it with his fingers. This detail relates directly to the clicking of castanets in Tchaikovsky's music, which starts up at the passage *con grazia* (bar 37), and continues till the final twelve bars marked *più mosso*. Of course, the introduction of castanets add a very Spanish flavour to this folkloric dance.[90] However, the rhythm employed (a beat followed by a triplet) is also suggestive of the noise of roasted cocoa beans spilling over onto a hard surface—a spilling which resonates visually with the little black dots of the buttons on the man's shirt and waistcoat.

The Arabian Dance

Petipa's scenario describes the Arabian dance as 'Coffee. Arabia, the kingdom of Yemen. Coffee Mocha. Oriental dance of 24 to 32 bars of sweet and enchanting music.'[91] The fact that the coffee here is specified as 'Mocha' coffee signifies that it comes via the port of Mocha, the principal port of the Yemen on the Red Sea in the first decades of the nineteenth century, famous for being a major marketplace for coffee. The costume designs show a group in Arab dress similar to that found in sketches of people from Morocco in the nineteenth century.[92] One man wears a fez, recalling the influence of the Ottoman Turks, and one woman wears a white veil, reminding the viewer that these people hail from Islamic lands. There seems nothing out of the ordinary about these people. However, the coffee dance is far from ordinary, and its music is not only 'sweet and enchanting', but its choreography also has an engaging allure.

The choreography of the Coffee dance (for a soloist and backing group of men and women) was originally written down in a Stepanov notation score in St Petersburg before the Russian Revolution of 1917, during the time when Nicolai Sergeev, *régisseur* and teacher of Stepanov notation, was employed there by the Imperial Theatres.[93] When he came to England in the 1930s he produced *The Nutcracker* for the fledgling Sadler's Wells Theatre in London. From Sergeev's time at Sadler's Wells further recordings of the ballet were made in Benesh notation.[94] A comparison of the recording of the solo part made in Benesh notation with the recording made in Stepanov notation shows general similarity, especially in the middle and final sections.

The Coffee solo is performed by a female artist. She enters on stage from upstage left and takes up a central lunge position *croisé*, facing diagonally downstage right, flanked on each side by the other dancers. Her hands are behind her head. Then, to a languorous 3/8 rhythm, punctuated by the subdued beat of a drum, she steps forwards into another lunge, this time *ouvert*, with her head towards the audience. She holds her position. She then steps forwards on the same line, changes the supporting foot and repeats the sequence to the other side. The sequence zigzags forwards towards the audience in this manner, seven times in all.[95] Are the zigzags merely as a succession of poses? Or what can be their import? It is true that there is no real dancing in this introduction, but there *is* allurement. If one conjures up a woman with a veil (as there is in the costume designs), with her face framed by her arms bent upwards at each side to allow her hands to be placed behind her head, then the emphasis is on the eyes which are not hidden by the veil. As her body, slowly but surely, oscillates diagonally downstage, her head and eyes are turned towards the front, remaining centrally fixed on the audience. She is, so to speak, drawing the audience in to her gaze. But why? In Islamic terms, the so-called '"eye of the heart" is the spiritual centre, the seat of the Absolute Intellect; illumination'.[96] Could the Coffee dance be about the mysteries of the mind? Certainly, in contrast to the Spanish dance, which is outwardly lively, the Arabian dance, from its inception, comes across as inwardly contemplative. In the middle section of the dance, turning steps are woven into the texture, accompanied by intermittent shakes from a tambourine which lend silvery sounds to the enchantment. In Islamic terms, the circle conveys 'the vault of heaven; divine light'.[97] It is, therefore, tempting to see these circular movements as traces of light from heaven. In any event, these circular movements of body and arms continue up until the end. The dance finishes with the approach of a cavalier, perhaps the man in the fez, who sits the dancer onto his right knee. Intriguingly, in the Benesh version, the dancer puts her hands across her eyes on the fourth bar from the end, just before she sits, only to pull them apart to shoulder level on the last bar.[98] Might this gesture be about the eyes alone, now hidden in the dark, now in the light, now blind, now seeing? Or are the hands in this gesture meant to part her veil to reveal her face at last (or to mimic the parting of a veil if there is none)? In Islamic symbolism, the veil 'represents veiled knowledge and revelation; revelation is the parting of the veil.'[99]

The Chinese Dance

Petipa's scenario describes the Chinese dance as 'Tea. 3/4 *allegretto* in Chinese fashion, small bells.'[100] The idea of 'tea' follows the other beverages, chocolate and coffee, and as Confiturembourg appears to be located in the Far East, then there is no better beverage than tea to represent that part of the world. Indeed, tea farms have been recorded as existing in China since 1000 BC. It was only much later, in the seventeenth century, that it was introduced into Russia when a quantity of it was gifted to the tsar.[101] As supplies became available in Russia, tea began to be drunk by larger numbers of people and it grew in popularity.[102] By the time of the ballet, it would have been considered as a home brew and is therefore an audience friendly choice. However, there is no sign of a teacup or samovar in the props associated with this dance. Instead, the ladies' costume designs sketch kimono-type dresses, mid-calf in length.[103] The figures wear platform shoes, with one holding a Chinese fan. As for the men, one is in a short-sleeved, blue-and-white tunic, he is bare-legged and wears a coolie hat, revealing a pigtail underneath.[104] The other man, much grander in appearance, has more the look of a Mongolian courtier, dressed in a long robe of deep cerise and orange, with lining of sky blue, and epaulettes of black and gold, turned up at the ends. He wears black boots turned up at the toe. Around his neck fall two, long strings of sky-blue beads and, on his pigtailed head, sits a gold-domed cap trimmed around the edge in dark fur and crowned with a small white sphere. [105] As mentioned above, hemispherical dome-shapes are, in Buddhism, symbolic of the heavens, and therefore the small white sphere here may imply a celestial/heavenly sphere.

Choreographically, the Chinese dance is staged for a line of four couples and a solo couple (perhaps the lady with the fan and the gentleman in the gold-domed cap). [106] A snippet of film survives from this dance's legacy in the Ballets Russes de Monte Carlo company's *Mariage d'Aurore, 1935-36*. [107] Here, two ladies in costumes like those described above, appear holding folding fans in one hand, while the other hand is clenched with index finger pointing upwards. They walk forwards (*emboîtés*) on point into an arabesque, and then rise and lower on point (*relevés*) around in a circle; they are followed by a pigtailed Chinaman in a coolie hat, like that of the bare-legged man described above; he comes into camera shot behind them, joyously prancing forwards from side to side, holding a parasol in one hand, while the other hand (like the ladies) is clenched with index finger pointing upwards. [108] The tenor of the steps from this snippet is very European and, indeed, it is unlikely that Petipa or Ivanov had any real knowledge of Chinese dancing. The clue to the meaning of the piece would seem to reside in the objects the dancers carry and what they do with them. For example, the ladies who fan their fans as they go may be invoking the Chinese fan symbolism of 'the power of the air which can infuse new life into the dead.' [109] This idea is particularly pertinent with regard to the previously stated belief of the inhabitants of Confiturembourg in metempsychosis. As for the man waving the parasol aloft above his head, he, like the little Moors with their parasols, may be invoking the parasol's symbolism as 'the canopy of the heavens' and its power, both temporal and spiritual. [110] Confiturembourg seems, more and more, to manifest a location somewhere between earth and heaven. As for the gestures of the dancers' fingers pointing upwards, it invites one to contemplate the above and beyond (with whatever spiritual implications that might garner). But maybe there is further choreographic meaning? An examination of the Stepanov score of the girl's solo part discloses a build-up of the rises on point (*relevés*), firstly on the spot, then in a circle, and, finally, pirouetting in the centre *sur place* eleven times before holding a finishing drawn-up position of the leg on point (*retiré*). [111] Although the man's pose is not notated for this final position, the fact that it isn't notated suggests that he is still there, supporting his partner. Moreover, if he is holding a parasol above his partner's head as she turns (ostensibly to protect her from the sun), then she becomes, in the view of the audience, the turning handle of the parasol. And the circular shade of the parasol (with its spokes) is symbolic of the sun (and its rays), and the parasol's long handle is symbolic of the cosmic axis linking heaven and earth. [112] This particular image, albeit a suggested possibility rather than a certitude, reinforces the notion of Confiturembourg as somewhere between heaven and earth. But, without doubt, the pirouetting finish of the female solo in the tea dance is not just another series of turns (*chaîné*) whirling across the diagonal in a flourish of bravura: it is performed head-on to the audience and does not travel, its rotating axis remaining rooted to the spot. It is a bold statement.

The Trepak

The next dance listed on Petipa's scenario is the trepak dance, detailed as a 'Trepak with hoop. Rapid 2/4'.[113] The libretto names it as a 'danse des bouffons' (fools' dance), and its presence here is traditional, as part of a royal entertainment which employed jesters as an amusement.[114] Tchaikovsky's orchestral score, on the other hand, describes it simply as a 'Russian dance'.[115] The trepak is a traditional Ukrainian dance, the music of which would have been known to a Russian audience (because of Russia's close, historical ties to the Ukraine).[116] No record of the dance's choreography survives, but a written reference can be found in the newspapers of the day where it was stated that a Mr Shiryaev 'adroitly jumped through a hoop' and showed off 'the vivacity and flexibility of his limbs'.[117] This short description ties up with the tumbling antics of a buffoon and is matched by the original costume design, penned 'fous' (fools, court jesters), which depicts a jester in a suit of golden yellow and black stripes.[118] The fool holds a circular hoop with small golden spheres attached on its inside circumference that would go round as the hoop revolved. The hoop can be read as a solar wheel, the wheel of life itself, and the accompanying music is so full of life and energy that this interpretation seems most fitting. But the wheel of life also includes death in its cycle, and this aspect is also hinted at in the black stripe of the jester's costume.[119]

The tricks and antics of the jesters are followed by a musical amusement called 'The Dance of the Mirlitons'.

The Mirlitons

The Mirlitons is described in Petipa's scenario as 'A dance of flutes, a polka tempo of 64 to 96 bars. They dance playing on their little pipes made out of reeds and covered at each end with a film of skin.' [120] The word 'mirliton', by the middle of the eighteenth century, meant a sort of short flute which was used on festive occasions (as it is here in the ballet), or as a children's toy. Traditionally, coloured paper was rolled around the flute in a decorative, spiralling pattern. [121] This general description corresponds to that given in the original costume design for the flute players in the ballet. [122] The sketch shows a female flautist playing a transverse flute, around which is a spiralling pattern of deep blue, bright gold and silvery white. This pattern is repeated on the tights, bodice and long tubular hat of the player. The overskirting of the tutu is white with a broad surround at the hem, of interlocking, triangular shapes of deep blue and gold. From the circular hem hang small, gold, pom-pom-like spheres. These spheres bring to mind the suns attached on the inner edge of the hoop in the trepak, except that they seem smaller. Perhaps they represent stars? The white overskirting is decorated all the way round at its outer edge with a golden musical stave with notes. The player has silver hair. On her right foot is a slipper of deep blue; on her left foot is a slipper of golden yellow. Prima facie, the flute player is simply a musician, festively attired. However, the spiral which clothes the player from head to toe symbolizes a different dimension. For,

> based on the direction of its spin, whether expanding outward and larger, or tightening inward and smaller,

a spiral is a cosmic symbol that may represent one or
the other of several dualities: growth or decay, ascent
or descent, evolution or involution, waxing or waning,
accumulation or dissolution, increasing or decreasing,
expanding or contracting [...] The double spiral com-
bines both opposites in one glyph. [123]

Could the vertical spiralling on the flute player represent
two spirals intertwined, the golden spiral representing solar
powers of growth and life, etc., and the contiguous deep-
blue and silver spiral representing lunar powers of decay and
death? And could their intertwining be a reflection of the
coexistence of life and death, and even (if one takes the me-
lodious music into the equation) a harmonious coexistence?
Certainly, if Confiturembourg is a hub for the process of metempsychosis, then the double spirals on the flute players'
costumes become relevant as symbols of the possible path-
ways involved in that process.

Fortunately, almost all of the original choreography
survives for 'The Mirlitons'. [124] It portrays a band of five
flautists (four with a soloist), who, like strolling players, pa-
rade around in symmetrical patterns, while playing their
flutes harmoniously. And, indeed, in Chinese tradition, the
flute is itself a symbol of harmony. [125] Punctuating these
manoeuvres are turns on-the-spot, during which the spiralling effect of their costumes, described above, comes
into play, swirling upwards and downwards simultaneously, embodying, one suspects, some sort of esoteric import.
But whatever it may convey, the dance of the Mirlitons is,
overall, a remarkable survival, engaging the spectator's eye

and ear with bright colour, harmonious melody and choreographic enchantment.

Mère Gigogne

The dance of Mère Gigogne is described in Petipa's scenario as:

> the dance of the thirty-two little clowns, led by Mère
> Gigogne and her little children emerging from un-
> derneath her skirt. 64 bars of 2/4 with a pronounced
> beat, not fast, which blend into 48 bars of 3/4 for the
> entry of Mère Gigogne and her children, who spring
> out from under her skirt, then a faster 2/4 — 32 to 48
> bars. At the finish, Mère Gigogne is in the middle of
> the group of clowns. [126]

Like the trepak, no precise record of this dance's original
choreography survives. But clues to its possible *raison d'être*
can be found in the original costume designs.

The character of Mère Gigogne derives from a theatrical
character created in 1602, an extremely large lady who wore
an enormous dress from under which came out a crowd of
children. [127] And the costume design for Mère Gigogne des-
ignates a tall woman in a colourfully florid, wide hooped
dress, wearing a white mob cap, *fichu* and large apron. [128] She
wears black-rimmed spectacles, and grey locks fall from beneath her mob cap. She is surrounded, not by little clowns,
but by little girls, all clothed in long pink dresses and bonnets
of the period. However, a note is set on the side which states,
'Remplacer les filletons par des polich[inelles]' (Replace the

little girls with little clowns.) So, for some reason, the presence of the little girls was ruled out at an early stage. As for
the little clowns, named as 'polichinelles' (figures of Punch
or Punchinellos) in the costume designs, they take after
Pulcinella, a character which originated in the *commedia
dell' arte*. The original costume design sketches a pot-bel-
lied hunchback, dressed in a pink-and-white striped suit
with cuffs, and wearing a thin tumbler hat with brim. [129] He
carries a long thin staff with a spiralled stripe of pink and
silver-edged white. This staff is reminiscent of a child's candy
stick but also doubles as some sort of baton for beating up
others. [130] And the traditional Pulcinella is known for being
belligerent. Indeed, 'Being self-centred and bestial, Pulcinella
had no scruples whatever, and because the moral suffering
from his physical deformity reacted upon his brain at the ex-
pense of his heart, he was exceedingly cruel.' [131] Given this
cruel nature of the character of Pulcinella, the question arises as to why this type should appear at all in this delightfully
innocent children's ballet. Even more curious is the colour
factor of pink and white, which relates the Punchinellos to
the colours of the costume of the Nutcracker Prince himself in this act. Oddly enough, the pink-and-white spiralled
staff which the Punchinello carries also harks back visually
to a barber's pole. But on the barber's pole, the colour red
symbolizes blood; could the pink of the Punchinello's staff
symbolize flesh instead? As for the white, it could take on
the symbolism of both life and death, for all flesh that lives
will also, one day, die. Moreover, the fact that the two colours are spiralled on a staff, brings back the symbolism of
the spiralled axis (already encountered in the costume of

the Mirlitons), which can 'depict winding and unwinding, birth and death.'[132] Furthermore, in the context of metempsychosis in Confiturembourg, the creation of physical life is alluded to here in the idea of the Punchinellos being born from under the skirts of Mère Gigogne. Are the pulchinellos meant to represent the naturally recurring rebirth into the world of war-like characters? Characters like Napoleon himself perhaps? But whatever one makes of the Punchinellos, they are not particularly pleasing to the eye with their pot bellies, hooked noses, and appearance like deformed dwarfs. It is, therefore, probably not surprising that their dance was omitted in the Stepanov score, which tells us that the piece had been cut.

The Waltz of the Flowers

Petipa's scenario sets out the Waltz of the Flowers as:

> The Waltz of the Flowers and Large Garlands. Eight bars of introduction, then the same number of bars as in the Villagers' Waltz in *The Sleeping Beauty* (second scene). The short gentleman claps his hands and thirty-six female dancers and thirty-six male dancers appear dressed as flowers, carrying a large bouquet, and present it to the fiancés. Having handed it over, the dancers, as is customary in operas, take their places and start to dance.[133]

The species of flowers presented to Claire and the Nutcracker Prince (who are now designated as fiancés) is specified in the French version of Petipa's scenario as being angelica flowers.[134]

However, angelica flowers are white, and the costumes of the flower dancers are, in the original costume designs, golden. [135] The sketch depicts a woman and a man in similar golden tunics with slightly belled-out skirts of orange, overlaid with golden stamens held down at their extremities with what look like round pearls. Large outer petals of gold are attached round their waists, those of the female curling upwards like petals in bloom, and those of the male reaching down to the edge of the skirt. The upper body garments are similar, but the female's take the form of a sleeveless bodice, and the male's take the form of a long-sleeved shirt. Both wear golden hats in the shape of a flower so that it covers the head and frames the face with a surround of large gold turned-up petals. Surrounds of golden petals also adorn the dancers' shoulders and the man's shirt cuffs. Together, they hold aloft a long garland of golden flowers. On their feet are golden slippers and what look like mid-calf stockings patterned with a flower motif and glass beads. The whole ensemble centres on the image of a golden flower, and that flower is most probably representative of a real sunflower. For sunflowers became popular as a cultivated plant in the eighteenth century in Russia, and by the early nineteenth century they had begun to be cultivated on an industrial scale for their oil. [136] The image of a sunflower would, therefore, have been welcomed by a Russian audience as something home-grown. Moreover, as growers of sunflowers know, the plant turns towards the sunlight, creating thereby a kind of natural metaphor for those who seek the light of truth. And that very seeking is appositely symbolized in Buddhism and Taoism as a 'golden flower.' 'Gold stands for light, the light of the mind itself; the flower represents the blossoming, or opening up, of the light of the mind. Thus the expression is emblematic of the basic awakening of the real self and its hidden potential.' [137] So it would appear that the significance of golden flowers is not to be passed over in the ballet as merely decorative, but indicative of spiritual rebirth. And as for the waltz itself, it cannot be dismissed lightly either, especially as it has over six and a half minutes allotted to its playing.

The original choreography for this waltz is recorded in the Stepanov score, and, like the Villagers' Waltz in *The Sleeping Beauty*, consists of mass manoeuvrings, in this case of *corps de ballet* and soloists, who travel in lines and curves, employing a mélange of steps, including *pas de basque, ballonnés* and waltzing. [138] Overall, the costumed dancers give the impression of a field full of circulating sunflowers. In the Taoist treatise, *The Secret of the Golden Flower*, it states that:

> The Golden Flower is the light. [...] When the light circulates, the energies of the whole body appear before its throne. [...] You only have to make the light circulate: that is the deepest and most wonderful secret. The light is easy to move but difficult to fix. If it is made to circulate long enough, then it crystallises itself; that is the natural spirit-body. [139]

Indeed, it is therefore through the circulation of light that inner rebirth is worked. In a later passage, it states: 'When the light is made to move in a circle, all the energies of heaven and earth, of the light and the dark, are crystallised. This is what is termed seed-like thinking, or purification of the energy, or purification of the idea. [...] Then suddenly there develops the seed pearl'.[140] The 'seed pearl' is the 'light' in crystallized form.[141] And here, one finds a possible reference to the pearls on the costumes. Mircea Eliade, in his analysis of *The Secret of the Golden Flower* and the imagery of crystallization effected by circulation, comments that:

> Several images serve to suggest the crystallisation of the Light: the Golden Flower which buds and opens, the seed that matures and becomes an embryo, or a pearl. These [...] metaphors converge and complete one another. The final result is the attainment of the Elixir of Immortality, symbolised by the Golden Flower.[142]

C G Jung, meanwhile, in his commentary on *The Secret of the Golden Flower*, remarks:

> The 'enclosure' or *circumambulatio*, is expressed in our text by the idea of a 'circulation'. The 'circulation' is not merely motion in a circle. But means, on the other hand, the marking off of the sacred precinct, and, on the other, fixation and concentration.[143]

Perhaps it is by the very length of the waltz (over six and a half minutes) that the audience are themselves drawn in to concentrate on the 'circulating' choreography and soak in, albeit unwittingly, its metaphor of a golden flower that opens in the light, resulting in spiritual, heavenly rebirth—a metaphor which contrasts strongly with the idea of physical, earthly rebirth which preceded it in the scene with Mère Gigogne and the Punchinellos.

The *Pas de Deux*

After the Waltz of the Golden Flowers comes the famous *pas de deux* for the Sugar Plum Fairy and her prince. Petipa's scenario gives the following details:

> *Pas de deux.* The Sugar Plum Fairy with Prince Orgeat [Coqueluche]. Adagio with colossal effects — 48 bars. Variation for the cavalier 6/8 — 48 bars. Variation for the ballerina, *piqué* 2/4-32 bars, during which the fall of water droplets from the fountains must be audible. Then to finish, 24 bars at a very rapid pace. Coda, another 88 bars—fast 2/4. [144]

In this prescription for the music of the *pas de deux*, the consort of the Sugar Plum Fairy is named as Prince Orgeat, the word 'orgeat' denoting barley sugar syrup. However, in the original costume designs, he is renamed 'Prince Coqueluche' with a note below reading 'N.B. Replace Prince Orgeat.' [145] The 'Coqueluche' designation is more enigmatic. It can mean 'contagious', as with diseases, and can refer to whooping cough. However, this analysis does not find credibility within the context of the ballet. More likely, is the attribution 'être aimé, admiré de', which would cast the prince as being loved and admired by the inhabitants of Confiturembourg. [146] In any event, he is depicted in the original costume designs wearing exotic, oriental-looking raiment. [147] A deep-turquoise-blue, long-sleeved tunic covers his upper body, complemented by deep-turquoise-blue boots. He wears plum-red leggings (which match the plum-red colour of the plums on the costume of the Sugar Plum

Fairy), which are overlaid with gold patterning, including a prominent gold star or sun covering the kneecap. A broad white waistband, divided by gold straps which slant upwards towards the breastbone and downwards at the waist, are decorated with blue turquoise stones. This waistband crimps in a sleeveless overtunic, diaphanous with veil-like qualities and punctuated with little gold dots (which match the little gold dots on the tutu skirt of the Sugar Plum Fairy). Around the prince's wrists are clamped gold wristbands studded with more large, blue turquoises. Two strings of large pearls hang around the prince's neck and smaller pearls edge the arm-holes of his tunic. On his head the prince sports three gold bands, attached to which are turquoise stones at the front, and, on the upper band, a pale-yellow plume which floats above his curly brown, short-cropped hair. Taken altogether, the colours making up the prince's appearance—brown, red, light yellow, white and blue, can be seen to correspond to the five Chinese elements of feng shui philosophy—wood, fire, earth, metal and water. [148] The veil-like overtunic, covered in tiny gold dots, like seeds, can be seen as the Buddhist 'veil of illusion', *maya*, which is the 'fabric from which the phe-nomenal world is woven'. [149] The golden star (or sun) on the kneecap, is, in Chinese culture, a symbol of 'the active force fertilising the earth'. [150] The prince, in this latter context, can be viewed as the male principle in creation, thereby render-ing his partner, the Sugar Plum Fairy (in her tutu bestrewn with golden 'seeds' and plums), the female principle in cre-ation. Interestingly, this role is backed up by another name given to the prince, 'Bienfaisant', which, in French, literally means 'well making', or 'widely making' or 'making much'. [151]

All these meanings could apply to the prince as a creator of earthly life, in line with the business of metempsychosis plied in Confiturembourg. The symbolism of the bluish-turquoise stones and large round pearls do not, however, convey worldly attributions. The blue, a colour of the heavens as well as of truth, complements the white pearls, which in China, are emblems of 'the spiritual essence of the universe'.[152] If one adds these last two factors to the symbolic make-up of the prince, then his faculties would seem to extend to both the earthly and the heavenly—a suitable circumstance for a prince whose territory of Confiturembourg appears to be situated somewhere between heaven and earth.

The Benesh choreographic record of the *pas de deux* for the Sugar Plum Fairy and Prince Coqueluche generally matches the Stepanov record and notates a predominance of circular and lozenge-like forms.[153] The circular forms mainly pertain to the arm positions and pirouettes of the ballerina and the promenades of her cavalier. The lozenge-like forms mainly pertain to a bent leg position (*retiré*), held and spun around (thereby visually creating the two sides of a lozenge), as well as to starting and finishing positions with feet together and legs bent (*pliés*), and held aerial positions of the ballerina with both legs bent and knees out to the side, outlining a lozenge. The circle, a universal symbol indicative of perfection, eternity and many other attributions, is, in Buddhism, a sign of the 'round of existence, enclosing all in the phenomenal world'.[154] The lozenge, as mentioned above, is a Western symbol of feminine fertility.[155] Here, the Sugar Plum Fairy who is making the 'lozenges' and whose tutu is covered in golden seeds alongside plums of various stages of growth, appears to personify fully the idea of fruitfulness which is synonymous with the lozenge. Her circling, however, is, in the *pas de deux*, aided or propelled by the actions of the prince. So both partners can be viewed as active participants in what comes across, symbolically, as an occult process in the round of phenomenal creation.

Towards the end of the *pas de deux* (bars 58-66), a puzzling piece of choreography occurs. [156] Roland Wiley has made the following assessment:

> In the last part, a mechanical device is introduced which is referred to in the CN [Sergeev choreographic score in Stepanov notation] as a *'reika'*. This seems to have been a track or guide along which a small platform travels; placed on the platform, a dancer can be drawn along the *reika* to give the illusion of gliding across the stage. After breaking the last pose of the preceding section, the Sugar Plum Fairy and her prince move 'to the *reika*' at the rear of the stage. Then they traverse the stage 'on the *reika*' from the audience's left to its right. This part of the dance is probably that depicted in the celebrated picture of Gerdt as Prince Coqueluche drawing Vavara Nikitina as the Sugar Plum Fairy on the surface of a shawl or cloth, as if by magic. [157]

Prima facie, this musical phrase, during which the ballerina (in the Stepanov notation) holds a pose on point (*attitude devant*), does not synchronize with the rest of the active dance. [158] In the picture of Gerdt and Nikitina referred to above by Wiley, Gerdt (costumed as Prince Coqueluche in the original costume designs) appears to pull Nikitina (costumed as the Sugar

Plum Fairy in the original costume designs) along on a long stretch of diaphanous material, one end of which is held up by Gerdt. The reason for this choice of material would seem to lie in its transparency, as it brings to mind a veil—a veil which triggers the Buddhist concept of 'the veil of illusion', called *maya*. If this material is meant to be *maya*, the 'fabric' from which the phenomenal world is 'woven', then this symphonic phrase in the ballet's accompaniment (which starts off loud, then becoming very loud) purports to illustrate a moment when seeds from the Sugar Plum Fairy come into contact with that 'fabric' and can, so to speak, germinate and take on an earthly existence. [159] It is, therefore, an important life-giving moment, which demands a loud *crescendo* to announce it. As the ballerina comes off the track, the music suddenly becomes soft, but builds again as the couple engage in more circular motions, bringing the *pas de deux* to a loud end.

There is no notation for the cavalier variation in the Stepanov score which is prescribed in Petipa's scenario to follow the *pas de deux*, but there is a notational script for the ballerina's variation.

The Dance of the Sugar Plum Fairy

The tune for the solo dance of the Sugar Plum Fairy, noted for its timbre of the celesta, is famous to this day. [160] Moreover, its original choreography was recorded not only in Stepanov notation, but also in Benesh, and these notations are well matched. [161] Indeed, the combination of sound and movement is delightful. But what might it mean? A leading clue could arise from an arm position in bar 21 of the Benesh recording, where both arms are crossed over in front, the hands bent back as the palms press downwards. This position is not classical, but *caractère*. [162] In fact, it is almost the same as in the mime of the Queen of the Wilis in *Giselle*, when she says, 'You will die!'. The word 'die' corresponds to this arm position, except that here, in *The Nutcracker*, the hands are not clenched. Nevertheless, the movement's reference to the idea of being buried in the ground is relevant. For the Sugar Plum Fairy, whose tutu is covered in golden seeds and sprouting plums of various sizes, must (in her role as the feminine creative principle) sow her seeds in the ground. [163] And, in fact, a great many of the arm movements (*port de bras*) consistently move through the position of the arms in front at skirt level (*bras bas*), up and outwards, which can easily be translated in the mode of *caractère* as the scattering out of the seeds seen on her tutu. The pressing down gesture of the hands can then be interpreted as a pressing down of the fallen seeds into the soil. When the tutu design changed later on, so that no seeds or tiny plums were in sight, then one would have expected the choreography to have been altered to adhere to the tenets of ballet classicism. However, this feature of the crossed over wrists seems to have avoided such alteration. As far as the positions of the legs and steps are concerned, two strands emerge. One strand relates to the lozenge symbol of fertility (mentioned above, constructed by alternating *retirés*), but this time in a solo setting. The other strand relates to classical steps which could well derive from ordinary *caractère* movements of the feet, used when planting in a garden. For example, the leg stretched out in front which flicks into the supporting leg twice, before stretching out again (*fondu*, two *petits battements devant*), if envisaged as *caractère*, conjures up a foot (shod in a dirty old garden shoe!) shifting the soil in and over a seed or around a seedling, and then, with a smaller inward movement, just topping it. Other classical steps, such as sliding steps, and steps involving change of weight (*glissades* and *pas de bourrée*), could relate to the smoothing over of soil and patting it down. In the final two bars (bars 51 and 52) of the Stepanov recording, the ballerina executes two 'lame ducks' (*tours piqués*) on the right diagonal, downstage, so that the left leg swings round from the back to the front, off the floor, just like the action of spreading out the icing on top of a cake evenly, or, here, raking over the top soil. Because the classicism of the dance which we see today can be envisaged as *caractère*, it is difficult to know how much of it could have been *caractère* originally, especially as the upper body movements in the Stepanov notation are almost entirely absent. [164] Nonetheless, its classical elements were likely to have been inspired by movements relating to the purpose of the role, which, as can be seen on the original costume design, involved a multiplicity of seeds.

The ballerina's solo is succeeded by two codas for the Sugar Plum Fairy and her cavalier, bringing the *pas de deux* section to its conclusion.

The Final Coda and the Apotheosis

The festive entertainment for Claire and the Nutcracker Prince is wound up with 'a general coda for all who are standing on the stage, together with those who have already danced. 128 bars 3/4, very fascinating and hectic.' [165] The libretto adds: 'Clara [Claire] is delighted with all that is

taking place before her eyes, and the Nutcracker Prince, ra-
diant with joy that he has been able to please his rescuer, tells
her fantastic tales about the Kingdom of the Sweets.'[166] At
the end of the final coda, comes the apotheosis. The ballet
master's scenario sets forth: 'Variously coloured fountains,
illuminating fountains, etc., etc. [...]. Grandiose *andante* of
16 to 24 bars.'[167] The libretto, on the other hand, dictates:
'The apotheosis represents a large beehive with worker bees
flying around it, vigilantly guarding their treasure.'[168] As
mentioned above with regard to Ivanov's designs, beehive
shapes of Greek tombs were suggestive of immortality, as
were bees themselves and honey in Western culture. Also
mentioned above, however, was the fact that the 'bee' was
a prominent symbol of the Emperor Napoleon, used on his
coronation robe, his great seal, etc. [...] So, although the ballet ends far from its beginnings in Napoleonic Bavaria, the
Napoleonic factor has not been left behind. And as Claire
and the Nutcracker Prince, both dressed in fashionable
clothes of the Napoleonic period, process in the apotheosis towards the large beehive, what did it suggest to the
audience? Are the couple destined for immortality, eternity,
liberation, Nirvana? or is it that the Napoleonic legacy in the
Russian psyche has another import?

Conclusion

There is no doubt that the balletic fantasy of *The Nutcracker* seems to take on a life of its own, but it is unlikely that the premise for it, was purely down to the imagination of those involved in its production. Already, historical fidelity to the time of Napoleon has been remarked upon. But was the location of Napoleonic Bavaria chosen simply because Nuremberg was famous for its wooden toys, such as the Nutcracker doll? It would appear not. For the Nutcracker doll, 'made in Nuremberg' and wearing a 'liberty cap', is not just a wooden toy, but flags up German feelings of liberty from French domination. Indeed, 'the German Romantics, intimidated by the French Revolution, defined German freedom as an inner state, not to be gained by French political violence. [...] The "German" position was a rebellion from social constraints on liberty, [...] a revolt that [...] only happened in the imagination.'[1] Given this position, the Nutcracker doll itself can now be seen as a talisman that, in displaying the 'cap of liberty', personifies this

'German' approach to liberty. The fact that the Nutcracker is wearing the cap on his head signifies that its symbolism of liberty is, appropriately, inward, in his head, in his mind and imagination. But why would such an approach be of interest to Russians in the late nineteenth century? It is true that nineteenth-century Russia looked to the West for ideas, but 'only on condition of not sacrificing its own moral authenticity.' [2]

> The Russians used German philosophical devices to build up their picture of the ideally fulfilling community of souls because [...] German discourse provided the most suitable foundations. [...] The simple Russian communal idea, for instance, corresponded to what the German Romantics had called 'the naïve.' The naïve was part of a mythological vision [...] intended to mark what the critical, modern, self-conscious mind had lost [...] and what it hoped to regain for happiness' sake. [...] A literary critic [...] once called it a paradise of resurrected naivety; the chance to live happily as a child again. [3]

And who can deny that the story of Claire and the Nutcracker Prince *is* a story of childhood naïvety, incorporating the communal life of Confiturembourg?

> When the Russians faced up to the idea of becoming a modern country, they did so conscious of the fact that they were choosing naivety as a quality they [...] had never lost. [...] The Russians had never relinquished their naïve state, and hoped they never would. They

wanted simple knowledge, the equivalent of not leaving the family and the village.[4]

When Claire and the Nutcracker Prince reach the small, rural community of Confiturembourg by boat, it would seem that this destination fits the naïve ideal of village life, yearned for by nineteenth-century Russians. But Confiturembourg is *not* their final destination. They move on towards the bees around the beehive, which, as emblems of Napoleon, augur a different future for them.

It is not known specifically why Napoleon chose the emblem of the bee to feature in his imperial trappings, but it has been suggested by historians that he chose them not only as representations of kingship, but also because bees represented order and diligence—attributes that were desirable to affix to his regime. The worker bees around the hive in the ballet, being eight students from the theatre school, were, most likely, lively bees, and perhaps they buzzed about busily as Claire and her prince approached.[5] What is certain is that the bee symbol was recognizable as being associated with French culture and the aftermath of the French Revolution (in the form of Napoleon's organized modernization programmes). Admittedly, in Napoleon's campaign of 1812, Russia had been the enemy, however:

Fighting an enemy produced a desire to study that enemy and all its national characteristics. The French Revolution, as part of recent French history, could not be ignored, since Napoleon was regarded by Russian officials 'first and foremost as a general of the French

Revolution.' Academic interest in modern European history was the offspring. During Alexander I's reign [1801-1825], courses in world history were taught at the universities of St Petersburg and Moscow. [6]

Moreover, the French Revolution became a subject of writers and scholarly publications. During the reign of Nicholas I (1825-1855), 'many foreign works and original Russian works about Napoleon were published in Russia.'[7] Moreover,

> the demand for an educated bureaucracy [...] compelled Nicholas' government to allow people to be at least acquainted with the French Revolution. [...] [And later, during the reign of Alexander II (1855-1881), and the beginning of the reign of Nicholas II (1894-1917)] the government needed to employ qualified people who knew Russia's enemies and allies as well. And it was France that became Russia's main ally by the end of the nineteenth century. [8]

This Russian motivation to have French-speaking diplomats explains the background behind the career of Ivan Alexander Vsevolojsky himself, who became a Russian diplomat, was well versed in the French language, and, as mentioned above, spent the years 1876-1881 at the Russian consulate in Paris. It is difficult to posit that he would not have been knowledgeable about the French Revolution.

After the death of Nicholas I in 1855, when controls over the universities were relaxed, 'the French Revolution was finally incorporated into the study of Modern European history. As soon as the French Revolution became a part of academic life, liberal intellectuals [...] began to rely on the French Revolution to substantiate their vision of Russia's political life.'[9] One such liberal was Maxim M Kovalevsky.[10] Kovalevsky was a sociologist who 'used the French Revolution primarily to demonstrate the negative effects of capitalist development on people.'[11] However, conversely, he was in favour of the growth of international trade which 'would bring about the economic integration of the whole world, eliminating the causes of war, and ultimately lead to a world federation of democratic states.'[12] It is this kind of liberal thinking that is envisaged in the different national dances in the second act of *The Nutcracker*, which are all linked to trading commodities. These dances follow the defeat of the Mouse King. And, as a personification of Napoleon, the Mouse King meets his Waterloo when Claire strikes him with her slipper. Historically, Napoleon's defeat at the battle of Waterloo in 1815 meant the collapse of the Continental Blockade set up by his regime and the resumption of normal, harmonious trading relations between countries.[13] The suite of national dances can, therefore, imply the collapse of this Continental Blockade. The Mouse King's defeat also implies, metaphorically, that Napoleon's system of capitalism and its benefits (mainly for his acolytes, the greedy mice) has collapsed too. In the ballet, the whole geography, having gone through a type of cleansing by means of the snow storm, resolves itself into the location of Confiturembourg, a small outpost which engages in international trade. This outpost is governed by a benevolent monarchy (the Sugar Plum Fairy and Prince Coqueluche), which regulates its people. This solution again blends into the liberal thinking of Kovalevsky. For he, in his study of French history leading up to the French Revolution, took the view that:

> the French monarchy had the option of appeasing the populace's material wants, and only the stupidity of the ruling elite prevented its implementation. [...] Kovalevsky implied [that] the French monarchy had a chance to attract the public to its side and prevent both its own downfall and the calamities of the revolution. The Russian *ancien régime* could employ elements of social structure of the Middle Ages (for example guilds) and put them in a new social-political context as the protector of the populace's interests. [14]

Kovalevsky also made a particular study of the Russian peasant commune, and he idealized the qualities of mutual support and the strong communal ties which epitomized it. In the ballet, the destination of the beehive with its busy bees would therefore appear, following Kovalevsky's ideals, to be a most suitable, almost timeless symbol for a productive, rural, peasant commune. But what role would Claire and the Nutcracker Prince play once they had arrived there? The obvious answer would seem to be that they are going to exercise the role of constitutional monarchs, a role which Kovalevsky and many other liberals of his day advocated. They would be, in Kovalevsky's terms, 'people's monarchs.'

> The 'people's monarch,' sensitive to the demands of the public, would not be bound to a small group of

well-to-do citizens, as was the case in a bourgeois republic. Soaring above all social groups, the people's
monarch would be in a position of power to intervene
on behalf of the populace. [...] Such a policy would
improve the populace's well-being while saving the
Russian monarchy from the Revolution. [15]

Kovalevsky, like many Russian liberal intellectuals, found in
the French Revolution and its outcomes a spur towards political liberation from absolute monarchy. Salvation for the
Russian populace would come from a 'people's monarchy.'
This vision of a Russian future for its people could well have
coincided with the political opinions of Vsevolojsky himself, who was a contemporary of Kovalevsky. However, as
Vsevolojsky's post at the Maryinsky Theatre was in the gift
of the tsar, it would not have been prudent for him to criti-
cize the Russian monarchy in any direct way. [16] Nevertheless,
this hypothesis of Russian liberalism which stems from *The
Nutcracker* ballet of 1892 is supported in commentaries of the
day. 'The high-calibre liberal generation which emerged from
the universities in the 1890s marked a unique, fleeting age in
Russia. The *émigré* philologist Roman Jakobson would later
look back on that decade as the summit of old Russian cultural achievement.' [17] And indeed, with regard to later events (not
least to the Russian Revolution itself), this Russian fin de siècle
situates itself as being finely balanced, a time when the ideas of
Russian liberals looked to the past to find a way forward, and
coalesced to some degree with the emerging ideas of Russian
radicals. [18]

But such political innuendoes which can be surmised

from *The Nutcracker* ballet would not have been in the mind of an audience in the 1890s. In the final moments of the work, all the spectators would have seen are the fiancés, innocently setting off for a large beehive where, presumably, they will live happily ever after.

Appendix

Russia, Romanticism and the East—A Brief Historical Glance

The Russian Federation is today a vast territory, incorporating different peoples and cultures, and which stretches from Saint Petersburg in the West to Vladivostok in the East. This link with the East began in the sixteenth century, when 'Russia mounted an expansive drive deep into the Far East, Central Asia, and the Caucasus that resulted in the formation of a Eurasian empire'.[1] By the beginning of the seventeenth century, however, this territory was still largely uncharted and little was known about its terrain. It was during the reign of Tsar Peter the Great, in the late seventeenth and early eighteenth century, that Dutch cartographers were first sent out to start mapping these conquered, Russian lands.[2] Moreover, the need for linguists who could speak the native tongues of these areas was important, and Peter the Great began to encourage Eastern studies, inviting leading European orientalists to join his newly established Academy of Sciences.[3] In the course of the eighteenth century, German explorers and scientists were to play a major part. They were to search for mineral resources, take scientific data and also catalogue ways and manners of indigenous peoples. In fact, it was the Germans who were the first to write about shamanism and make it known to the Russians themselves. [4] During this period of the Enlightenment, however, with its emphasis on rationalism and scepticism, findings about the magical rituals and shamanic dream states of shamanism were not taken seriously. It was only with the advent of Romanticism that European scholars and writers became interested in tribal, spiritual beliefs and began searching for their origins in the East. Prominent among such scholars, was Friedrich Schlegel, who promulgated the idea that India laid the foundations of Western civilizations. [5] He argued that shamanism itself, had spread north from India and was, in his opinion, a 'degenerated northern version of classical Oriental beliefs,' i.e., Buddhism. [6] Then there was Johann Gottfried Herder, who promoted the role of the imagination. [7] 'To Herder, the ability of shamans to reach out and captivate their audiences pointed to the "victories of the imagination".' [8] Other, early Romantic scholars, such as Friedrich Schelling, influenced by the Romantic mythical image of India, not only validated the imaginary and visionary, but elaborated on the view of surrounding nature as a living entity. [9] And it was the German philosophers like Schelling, with their culture of German idealism, that had a profound influence on Russia. Indeed, many Russians travelled to hear Schelling speak, and his Russian disciples adopted his ideas of natural philosophy. [10] According to Schelling, God was present in nature, and through the contemplation/dreaming of nature, lay the means to transcend the ordinary and gain insight into the ever-present spirit world. [11] This viewpoint ties in with the ideas of Gotthilf Schubert, a student of Schelling, who took a particular interest in the fusion of nature and religion in the culture of ancient India. [12] He stated:

> In the same way as the environment relays back to man from all quarters a radiant image of his own physical existence, so also is reflected an image of his intimate, spiritual life. [13]

and

> The Word of nature, or rather God having become nature, was for Antiquity, at the same time, a dream and the explanation of that dream. [14]

Moreover, Schubert's Romantic, animated conception of nature has some similarities with shamanic beliefs, where 'all phenomena of nature, including human beings, plants, animals, rocks, rain, thunder, lightning, stars and planets, and even tools, are animate, imbued with a life essence or soul'. [15] Schubert's works were read in Russia, where he was especially admired by Fyodor Golubinsky, a professor at the Moscow Theological Academy and a gifted expositor of German idealism. [16] But of all the German Romantic authors, it is E T A Hoffmann who had the most influence. [17] From 1822 onwards, his works were translated and published in Russia. 'Nussknacker und Mausekönig' itself came out initially in 1835, 1840 and 1843, and then featured in a complete edition of Hoffmann's works in 1873. And around

1893, 'a revival started [...] with major editions of Hoffmann's writings and his espousal by the symbolists' [18]—this dating of a Hoffmann revival coinciding directly with the premiere of *The Nutcracker* ballet in December, 1892.

At the same time as early European Romanticists' views on the Orient were influencing Russian scholars at the beginning of the nineteenth century, Russia was consolidating its hold on territories in Asia. Ever mindful of the practical need for linguists, Kazan University had been founded in 1804. [19] Later, in 1833, a department of Oriental languages was established, which was largely the brainchild of Count Sergei Uvarov. [20] Uvarov had spent time in Europe in the first decade of the nineteenth century, reading the works of the European Romanticists and meeting them. He, like his contemporaries, believed that India was the cradle of civilization, giving rise to the Classical world of Greece and Rome, and then to Augustine, Aquinas, Descartes and Leibniz. [21] He advocated a renaissance of Oriental studies, publishing in 1810 an essay entitled, *Projet d'un académie asiatique* (Project for an Asian Academy). He became the superintendent of education for the district of St Petersburg in that same year and a member of the Russian Academy of Sciences in 1811 (becoming its President in 1818). In 1832 he became Deputy Minister of Public Education.

His policies both as President of the Academy of Sciences and as educational minister, resulted in Russia's emergence as an international center of oriental scholarship, an esteem the country holds to this day. Indeed, Uvarov brought to Russia the main heritage of the Oriental Renaissance—to recognise and study the East as an essential contributor to world civilisation, [...] and to create a self-perpetuating school of scholarly research on the topic. [22]

During the 1840s, learned societies began to develop in Russia, with sections focusing on oriental studies. In 1854, the Faculty of Oriental Languages at Kazan was relocated to the University of St Petersburg, along with most of its staff and library. The Ministry of Education thought that such a move would encourage the recruitment of more Russian students. In 1863, Vasilii Grigor'ev became its first professor of the history of the East. [23] Grigor'ev had already, from the 1840s, been playing a leading part in linking research in oriental studies to the Russian elite's quest for national and imperial identities, and he would continue to do so till the 1870s. [24] Significantly, it was around this time that translations of the main works of the German philosopher Leibniz, who had studied and written on Chinese Confucianism, were published in St Petersburg (1868-71) and were used extensively in the teaching of philosophy. [25] Another leading figure at St Petersburg University was Victor Romanovich Rozen, who joined its Faculty of Oriental Studies in 1872, later becoming a professor and dean from 1893-1902. [26] 'Rozen played a crucial part in completing the "nationalisation" of Russian Oriental studies while achieving its simultaneous internationalisation.' [27] Rozen perceived Russia as multi-ethnic and going through a process of cultural integration. An important contemporary of Rozen was Wilhelm Radloff, a German who came to work in Russia and who is credited as being the founder of Turkology, a scientific study of Turkic peoples.[28] Radloff became interested in the native peoples of Siberia while working as a schoolteacher in Barnaul, in the south-west of Siberia.[29] He took the Russian name Vasilii Vasilievich Radlov, and in the 1860s till the 1890s he published works on ethnography in Germany and Russia, including his influential book, *Aus Sibirien* (From Siberia), published in 1884. Notably, he became one of the leading authorities on shamanism and was able to reconstruct a picture of native Siberian spirituality that far surpassed many contemporary accounts. He also helped establish the Russian Museum of Ethnography and became director of the Asiatic Museum in St Petersburg from 1884-1894. His time at the Asiatic Museum coincides with the 1892 premiere of *The Nutcracker*. The Museum could have been a resource for the oriental costumes which appear in the final act of the ballet.

Finally, we must note that, along with Russian colonization and interest in Asiatic peoples in the nineteenth century, the coming of the Trans-Siberian Railway made these regions and cultures much more accessible. The railway, which ran from Moscow to Vladivostok and was inaugurated in 1890, was built between 1891 and 1916.[30] Its very coming into existence must have stimulated people's interest and imagination towards the Orient. *The Nutcracker* ballet, with its own imaginative oriental vista, is very much a work of its time.

Endnotes

Introduction

[1] Ivan Alexandrovich Vsevolojsky (1835-1909); Marius Ivanovich Petipa (1818-1910); Lev Ivanovich Ivanov (1834-1901); Peter Ilyich Tchaikovsky (1840-93); Mikhail Ilyich Bocharov (1831-95); Konstantin Matveyevich Ivanov (1869-1916).

[2] The oldest choreographic score is located today among the Nicolai Sergeev dance notations (MS Thr 245) in the Harvard Theatre Collection, Harvard University, Cambridge, Massachusetts. Written in Stepanov notation, it records stage patterns and steps almost exclusively, but is short on arm and head movements. However, where there is other evidence, either in notational form or on film and which matches these Stepanov writings, then this more complete record has been consulted for the purposes of this text.

[3] Ernst Theodor Hoffmann (1776-1822). 'The Nutcracker' was originally published in Berlin in German under the title 'Nussknacker und Mausekönig', in Kinder-Mährchen (Berlin, 1816). Alexandre Dumas (1802-70). Dumas' version of 'The Nutcracker' was published in Paris in French under the title Histoire d'un casse-noisette in 1845.

[4] Maria Carlson, No Religion Higher than Truth. A History of the Theosophical Movement in Russia, 1875-1922 (Princeton, New Jersey: Princeton University, 1993), p. 21. Knowledge of foreign languages grew in Russia during the second half of the nineteenth century, especially French. Cf. Dmitry Shlapentokh, The French Revolution in

Russian Intellectual Life (New Brunswick New Jersey: Transaction Publishers, 2009), p. 122.

[5]   Tsar Alexander III (1845-94), tsar from 1881 till 1894; Tsar Nicholas II (1868-1917), tsar from 1894 till 1917; Tsarina Alexandra Feodorovna (1872-1918). Cf. Joanny Bricaud, 'Le Mysticisme à la Cour de Russie', in *Etudes Traditionelles* (Paris, 1921), p. 18.

[6]   Cf. Roland John Wiley, *Tchaikovsky's Ballets. Swan Lake, Sleeping Beauty, Nutcracker* (Oxford: Clarendon, 1985), p. 10.

[7]   Marius Petipa was born into a family of dancers and gained valuable experience studying with his father in his youth. He made his debut in Brussels in 1831, and thereafter danced in different countries including France, North America and Spain. It was as a dancer that he took up a position in St Petersburg in 1847. He graduated to duties as a ballet master, becoming first ballet master there in 1862.

Act I, Scene I

[1]   The Treaty of the Confederation of the Rhine was signed in Paris in 1806 by sixteen German states which joined together in a confederation. One of these states was Bavaria. By the Treaty of Pressburg in the previous year, Bavaria had become a kingdom.

[2]   Cf. Alexandre Dumas, *Histoire d'un casse-noisette* (Paris: J Hetzel, 1845), vol. 1, p. 19.

[3]   The design by Ivanov is photographed in an article, 'Casse-Noisette', in *About the House*, vol. 2, no. 8, Christmas 1967, p. 8. Cf. plate no. 23.

[4]   With the opening up of new sea routes and the discovery by Europeans of new lands around the globe, it became popular from the seventeenth century onwards, for those with means, to collect exotic specimens.

[5]   Cf. Dumas, *Histoire d'un casse-noisette*, p. 15; and Hoffmann's 'Nussknacker und Mausekönig', p. 115, where the family are named as 'Stahlbaum', which literally means 'tree of steel'. All translations mine.

[6]   The porcelain on display on top of the cabinet is reminiscent of Delftware, a blue and white pottery made by the Dutch in Delft but inspired by Chinese porcelain. Original blue and white porcelain imported from China in the early seventeenth century could only be afforded by the very rich.

[7]   Cf. Jean Chevalier and Alain Gheerbrant, *Dictionary of Symbols*

(London: Penguin, 1996), pp. 621, 1034.

8   J C Cooper, *An Illustrated Encyclopaedia of Traditional Symbols* (London: Thames & Hudson, 1978), p. 180.

9   Sarah Tricha, *Origins and Meanings of the Eight-Point Star*, at <www.moroccoboard.com/features/92-sarah-tricha/821-origins-and-meanings-of-the-eight-pointed-star>, accessed 15 May 2013.

10 Cf. Wiley, *Tchaikovsky's Ballets*, p. 376. Cf. J E Cirlot, *A Dictionary of Symbols* (Mineola, New York: Dover, 2002), p. 37. The image of a large, single candelabra appears in the 1845 Dumas publication of *Casse-noisette*, p. 41, in an illustration by Bertall.

11 Peter Tchaikovsky, *Casse-noisette*, orchestral score, libretto and scenario of Marius Petipa (Moscow: State Music Publishing, 1955), vol. 2, p. 295. All translations mine.

12 Cf. Wiley, *Tchaikovsky's Ballets*, p. 334.

13 J H Philpot, *The Sacred Tree* (London: Macmillan, 1897), p. 167.

14 Lyndy Abraham, *A Dictionary of Alchemical Imagery* (Cambridge: CUP, 1998), p. 150.

15 Ibid., p. 82.

16 Theatre Library of St Petersburg, sketches folder 1463/1-20, no. 1.

17 Ibid., no. 2.

18 Ibid., nos. 9-17, marked 'Merveilleuses' and no. 6, marked 'Merveilleuses et Incroyables.'

19 Hoffmann, 'Nussknacker und Mausekőnig', p. 115, and Dumas, *Histoire d'un casse-noisette*, vol. 1, p. 16. The attributions given to Silberhaus are ambiguous, for the words 'docteur' and 'président' could apply to a doctor of law as well as to a doctor of medicine. However, the attribution 'président' could equally apply to a magistrate or to, say, the president of a scientific association.

20 Cf. *Au temps des Merveilleuses: La Société parisienne sous le Directoire et le Consulat* (Paris: Musée Carnavalet, 2005), p. 4.

21 Theatre Library of St Petersburg, sketches folder 1463/1-20, no. 33.

22 Jean-Auguste-Dominique Ingres (1780-1867). Cf. Odile Nouvel-Kammer, *Napoleon and the Art of the Empire Style 1800-1815* (New York: Abrams, 2007), p. 335.

23 Cf. <www.oakthriftumbrellas.com/pages/umbrellas4.htm>, accessed 5 January 2013.

24   Choreographic score in Stepanov notation of *The Nutcracker*, Harvard Theatre Collection, MS Thr 245. Cf. <Pds.lib.harvard.edu/pds/view/45336942>, plan 3 of electronic sequence page 12, accessed 3 December 2013.

25   Ibid., plan 6. All translations mine.

26   Peter Ilyich Tchaikovsky, *Casse-Noisette*, piano reduction (Moscow: P Jurgenson, 1892), p. 10. All translations mine. Cf. plate no. 9.

27   <en.wikipedia.org/wiki/Tempus_fugit>, accessed 1 December 2012.

28   Cf. Chevalier and Gheerbrant, *Dictionary of Symbols*, p. 729.

29   Cf. Tchaikovsky, *Casse-noisette*, piano reduction, p. 10.

30   Tchaikovsky, *Casse-noisette*, orchestral score, libretto and scenario of Marius Petipa, vol. 1, p. 33.

31   Cf. Dr Florian Kiuntke, '1886—Winter Palace in St Petersburg ablaze with electric light', at <www.siemens.com/history/en/news/1055_winter-palace.htm>, accessed 11 October 2013.

32   Cooper, *An Illustrated Encyclopaedia of Traditional Symbols*, p. 177.

33   In the original Hoffmann tale as well as the Dumas version, the daughter of the Silberhauses is named Marie.

34   The governess in the Dumas version, is called Mademoiselle Trudchen. Cf. Dumas, *Histoire d'un casse-noisette*, vol. 1, pp. 18-19.

35   Cf. photo no. 17 (Collection of the Bakhrushin State Theatre Museum, Moscow), in Roland John Wiley, *The Life and Ballets of Lev Ivanov* (Oxford: Clarendon, 1997).

36   Cf. illustration by Bertall in Dumas, *Histoire d'un casse-noisette*, vol. 1, p. 19.

37   The symbol of 'Marianne' lasts to this day in France.

38   Tchaikovsky, *Casse-noisette*, piano reduction, p. 21.

39   Cf. plate no. 2.

40   Dumas, *Histoire d'un casse-noisette*, vol. 1, pp. 35-6.

41   Cf. ibid., p. 14.

42   Theatre Library of St Petersburg, sketches folder 1463/1-20, no. 23. Cf. plate no. 1. Note that the style of Claire's dress is later in fashion to that of the Bertell illustrations in the Dumas publication of 1845. Cf. plate nos. 2, 14.

43   Dumas, *Histoire d'un casse-noisette*, vol. 1, p. 93. Cf. plate no. 2.

44   Theatre Library of St Petersburg, sketches folder 1463/1-20, no. 28.

In the Bertall illustrations of the Dumas publication of 1845, Fritz and his friends are clothed in shirts and knee breeches, typical of the mid-eighteenth century. Cf. plate no. 2. The long-trousered garb in the ballet designs again indicates the Napoleonic era.

45 Frederick the Great (1712-86), King of Prussia from 1740 till his death.

46 Cf. plate no. 5, detail taken from the Bertall illustration in Dumas, *Histoire d'un casse-noisette*, vol. 1, p. 44.

47 Cf. Tchaikovsky, *Casse-Noisette*, piano reduction, p. 17.

48 Tchaikovsky, *Casse-noisette*, orchestral score, libretto and scenario of Marius Petipa, vol. 2, p. 297.

49 Quoted in Wiley, *The Life and Ballets of Lev Ivanov*, p. 139. The choreography of this dance, as well as the choreography of the majority of all other dances in the ballet, has not survived intact.

50 Ibid.

51 Marie Petipa (1857-1930); Vera Petipa (1885-1961). Theatre Library of St Petersburg, sketches folder 1463/1-20, no. 8. The sketch is marked 'Petipa I & II', indicating that it is for both Marie and Vera Petipa.

52 In 1806, Maximilian Joseph, Elector of Bavaria, was made King of Bavaria. At this juncture, Napoleon arranged for his stepson, Eugène de Beauharnais, to marry Maximilian's daughter Auguste Amalie.

53 Quoted in Wiley, *The Life and Ballets of Lev Ivanov*, p. 139.

54 Tchaikovsky, *Casse-noisette*, orchestral score, libretto and scenario of Marius Petipa, vol. 2, p. 295.

55 Dumas, *Histoire d'un casse-noisette*, vol. 1, p. 22. In the original Hoffmann tale of 'Nussknacker und Mausekönig', Drosselmayer is a chief law officer. However, Dumas' designation of Drosselmayer as a 'doctor' could graft well with Président Silberhaus, also designated by Dumas as 'doctor', if they were both 'medical' doctors.

56 Cf. Dumas, *Histoire d'un casse-noisette*, vol. 1, pp. 24-5.

57 Cf. <en.wikipedia.org/wiki/Meyer_(surname)>, accessed 16 September 2013.

58 Theatre Library of St Petersburg, sketches folder 1463/1-20, no. 3. Cf. plate no. 3.

59 Cf. Dumas, *Histoire d'un casse-noisette*, vol. 1, p. 22. Cf. plate no. 4.

60 Ibid.

61 Tchaikovsky, *Casse-noisette*, piano reduction, p. 29.

[62] Cf. <http://en.wikipedia.org/wiki/Snuff_(tobacco)>, accessed 30 December 2012.

[63] Rosalind Savill, *The Wallace Collection. French Gold Boxes* (London: Wallace Collection, 1991), introduction.

[64] Choreographic score in Stepanov notation of *The Nutcracker*, Harvard Theatre Collection, MS Thr 245. Cf. <Pds.lib.harvard.edu/pds/view/45336942>, plan 3 of electronic sequence page 8, accessed 12 March 2014.

[65] In today's culture, snuff sniffing is no longer practised and, if included in a production, could be misconstrued as drug consumption. However, in Russia, in the late nineteenth century, although the habit was dying out, Carl Fabergé, jeweller to the tsar, continued to make very expensive snuff boxes which were very acceptable as gifts.

[66] Tchaikovsky, piano reduction of *Casse-noisette*, p. 32.

[67] Tchaikovsky, orchestral score of *Casse-noisette*, orchestral score, libretto and scenario of Marius Petipa, vol. 2, p. 297.

[68] 'Of Cauliflowers and Kings', in *New English Review*, at <www.newenglishreview.org/blog_email.cfm/blog_id/24999>, accessed 17 November 2013.

[69] Tchaikovsky, orchestral score of *Casse-noisette*, orchestral score, libretto and scenario of Marius Petipa, vol. 2, p. 297.

[70] Cf. ibid., p. 295.

[71] Theatre Library of St Petersburg, sketches folder 1463/1-20, no. 5. Cf. plate no. 6.

[72] Ibid., no. 6.

[73] Maximilian Joseph, Prince-Elector of Bavaria (1799-1805), King of Bavaria (1806-1825).

[74] Napoleon was First Consul from 1800 till 1804, when he became Emperor.

[75] Cf. John H. Gill, *With Eagles to Glory* (London: Greenhill, 1992), pp. 64-5.

[76] Interest in automata peaked from 1860-1910 and therefore, they would have been topical for a Russian audience at the premiere of *The Nutcracker*.

[77] Dumas, *Histoire d'un casse-noisette*, vol. 1, p. 23.

[78] Ibid., p. 42, and Hoffmann, 'Nussknacker und Mausekönig', p. 118.

79 Cf. Dorinda Outram, *Panorama of the Enlightenment* (Los Angeles: J Paul Getty Museum, 2006), p. 24.

80 Julien Offray de La Mettrie, *Man a Machine* (La Salle, IL: Open Court, 1912), p. 93. Julien Offray de La Mettrie (1709-51), French physician and philosopher.

81 William Clark, Jan Golinski and Simon Schaffer (eds.), *The Sciences in Enlightened Europe* (London: University of Chicago, 1999), p. 268.

82 Ibid., p. 269.

83 Tchaikovsky, *Casse-noisette*, orchestral score, libretto and scenario of Marius Petipa, vol. 2, p. 298.

84 Theatre Library of St Petersburg, sketches folder 1463/1-20, no. 8.

85 Ibid., no. 7.

86 The figures of the *commedia dell' arte*, at least since the eighteenth century when Italian troupes started coming to Russia, were well known to the Russians. The theme was used at the Maryinsky Theatre in 1899 for the ballet *Harlequinade*. Cf. J Douglas Clayton, *'Pierrot' in Petrograd* (Montreal: McGill-Queen's University, 1993).

87 Napoleon conducted his first Italian campaign in 1796-7, his second in 1799-1800. By the Treaty of Pressburg in 1805, the then Republic of Venice was given over to the infant Kingdom of Italy.

88 The tradition of carnival was revived in 1979. Cf. <en.wikipedia.org/wiki/Carnival_of_Venice>, accessed 24 November 2013.

89 Cf. Frederick C Schneid, *Soldiers of Napoleon's Kingdom of Italy* (Oxford: Westview, 1995), pp. 79-89.

90 Pierre Louis Ducharte, *The Italian Comedy* (New York: Dover, 1966), p. 134.

91 Schneid, *Soldiers of Napoleon's Kingdom of Italy*, p. 60.

92 Ibid., p. 64.

93 Hoffmann, 'Nussknacker und Mausekönig', pp. 124, 162.

94 Dumas, *Histoire d'un casse-noisette*, vol. 1, pp. 44, 85.

95 Cf. ibid., pp. 76, 87.

96 Tchaikovsky, *Casse-noisette*, orchestral score, libretto and scenario of Marius Petipa, vol. 2, p. 295.

97 Tchaikovsky, *Casse-noisette*, piano reduction, p. 38.

98 Theatre Library of St Petersburg, sketches folder 1463/1-20, nos. 3, 4. Cf. plate nos. 3, 8.

99   Hoffmann, 'Nussknacker und Mausekőnig', p. 132.

100   Dumas, *Histoire d'un casse-noisette*, vol. 1, p. 48.

101   Ibid. The French phrase is, 'un mauvais petit bonnet de montagnard'. Cf. plate no. 7.

102   Ibid.

103   Cf. <en.wikipedia.org/wiki/Phrygian_cap>, accessed 18 November 2012. The origin of the Phrygian cap as a symbol of freedom from tyranny goes back to Republican Rome.

104   Polish recruits in Napoleon's armies reached many thousands and came mainly from the peasantry. They formed separate Polish units under French command. Many Poles believed that Napoleon would come to their aid against Prussia, Austria and Imperial Russia. They fought with Napoleon's armies against the Russians in 1812, but were defeated.

105   Poland did not regain its independence until the end of World War I in 1918.

106   Cf. Dumas, *Histoire d'un casse-noisette*, vol. 1, p. 48.

107   Tchaikovsky, *Casse-noisette*, piano reduction, p. 38.

108   Cirlot, *A Dictionary of Symbols*, p. 282.

109   Richard Folkard, *Plant Lore, Legends and Lyrics* (London: Sampson Low & Co., 1884), p. 463.

110   Tchaikovsky, *Casse-noisette*, piano reduction, p. 42.

111   Choreographic score in Stepanov notation of *The Nutcracker*, Harvard Theatre Collection, MS Thr 245. Cf. <Pds.lib.harvard.edu/pds/view/45336942>, electronic sequence page 41, opening stave line, bars 4-6, accessed 12 March 2014.

112   Tchaikovsky, *Casse-noisette*, piano reduction, pp. 47-9.

113   Ibid., p. 49.

114   This first verse for this tune was written in 1794 by Klamer Eberhard Karl Schmidt (1746-1824). It was published in Berlin in 1802. Cf. <www.volksliederarchiv.de/text889.html>, accessed 1 September 2013. All verse translations mine.

115   The remaining verses were written in 1812 by August Friedrich Ernst Langbein (1757-1835). They were published in 1813. Cf. <www.gedichte.xbib.de/Langbein_gedicht_Das+Gro%DFvaterlied.htm>, accessed 1 October 2013.

116   Bavaria did not switch sides till the autumn of 1813.

[117] The first battle of Polotsk took place in August 1812, the second battle of Polotsk in October 1812.

[118] Quoted in Wiley, *The Life and Ballets of Lev Ivanov*, p. 139.

[119] Cf. <library.ndsu.edu/grhc/articles/magazines/german/seebach.html>, accessed 1 December 2013.

[120] Count Peter Christianovich Wittgenstein (1769-1843). Cf. <en.wikipedia.org/wiki/Peter_Wittgenstein>, accessed 1 December 2013.

[121] Choreographic score in Stepanov notation of *The Nutcracker*, Harvard Theatre Collection, MS Thr 245. Cf. <Pds.lib.harvard.edu/pds/view/45336942>, electronic sequence page 40, plan 2, accessed 12 March 2014.

[122] Tchaikovsky, *Casse-noisette*, piano reduction, p. 47.

[123] Ibid.

[124] Emile Gevaert, quoted in Chevalier and Gheerbrant, *Dictionary of Symbols*, p. 883.

[125] Tchaikovsky, *Casse-noisette*, piano reduction, p. 50.

[126] Mesmerism was pioneered by Franz Anton Mesmer (1734-1815).

[127] Thomas Street Millington, *A Lecture on the Phenomena of Dreams, Mesmerism, Clairvoyance* (London: Boiler, 1852), pp. 24-5.

[128] Ibid., p. 25.

[129] Cf. ibid., p. 37.

[130] Tchaikovsky, *Casse-noisette*, piano reduction, p. 50.

[131] Quoted from the libretto of *The Nutcracker*, in Wiley, *Tchaikovsky's Ballets*, p. 335. Cf. plate no. 10.

[132] La Mettrie, *Man a Machine*, p. 135.

[133] Beryl Rowland, *Birds with Human Souls* (Knoxville: University of Tennessee, 1978), p. 118.

[134] The character of Drosselmayer does not, contrary to what happens in many modern productions of *The Nutcracker*, reappear in the original version of the ballet.

[135] *La Symbolique du Rêve* was published by Kunz in April 1814, two years before Hoffmann's 'Nussknacker und Mausekönig', also published by Kunz. Gotthilf Heinrich von Schubert (1780-1860). Carl Friedrich Kunz de Bamberg (1785-1849).

[136] Gotthilf Heinrich Schubert, *La Symbolique du Rêve* (Paris: Albin Michel, 1982), p. 64. All translations mine.

[137] Ibid., p. 100.

[138] Tchaikovsky, *Casse-noisette*, piano reduction, p. 52.

[139] Schubert, *La Symbolique du Rêve*, p. 110.

[140] Ibid., p. 76. N.B. the 'Unknown Philosopher' cited here denotes Louis-Claude de Saint-Martin (1743-1803), French philosopher.

[141] Cf. ibid., p. 168.

[142] Cf. Heinrich Jung-Stilling, quoted in Andreas B Kilcher and Philipp Thiesohn (eds.), *Die Enzyklopädik des Esoterik* (München: Wilhelm Fink, 2010), p. 267.

[143] Cf. Schubert, *La Symbolique du Rêve*, p. 134.

[144] Victor Girard, *La Transmigration des Ames* (Paris: Perrin, 1888), pp. 55-6. Translation mine.

[145] Tchaikovsky, *Casse-noisette*, piano reduction, p. 54.

[146] Tchaikovsky, *Casse-noisette*, orchestral score, libretto and scenario of Marius Petipa, vol. 2, p. 299.

[147] Cf. Joanny Bricaud, 'Le Mysticisme à la Cour de Russie', pp. 14-15.

[148] Schubert, *La Symbolique du Rêve*, p. 79.

[149] Cf. Ibid., p. 31.

[150] Zofia Ameisenowa, 'The Tree of Life in Jewish Iconography', in *Journal of the Warburg Institute* (1938-9), no. 2, p. 337.

[151] Chevalier and Gheerbrant, *Dictionary of Symbols*, p. 1033.

[152] Tchaikovsky, *Casse-noisette*, orchestral score, libretto and scenario of Marius Petipa, vol. 2, p. 295.

[153] Theatre Library of St Petersburg, sketches folder 1463/1-20, nos. 47-9.

[154] Cf. <en.wikipedia.org/wiki/Hammeau_de_la_Reine>, accessed 13 December 2013. Marie Antoinette (1755-93), became Queen of France in 1774.

[155] Theatre Library of St Petersburg, sketches folder 1463/1-20, no. 52.

[156] Cooper, *An Illustrated Encyclopaedia of Traditional Symbols*, p. 79.

[157] Tchaikovsky, *Casse-noisette*, orchestral score, libretto and scenario of Marius Petipa, vol. 2, p. 295.

[158] Theatre Library of St Petersburg, sketches folder 1463/1-20, nos. 55, 56.

[159] Cf. plate nos. 11, 12.

[160] Gingerbread was, and still is, known in German as 'Lebkuchen'. Cf. <en.wikipedia.org/wiki/Lebkuchen>, accessed 29 November 2012.

[161] Gingerbread products take a prominent place at Christmas fairs in Germany and Austria to this day.

[162] The leader of the Tyrolean rebellion against Napoleon was Andreas Hofer (1767-1810). He was an innkeeper who organized local militia forces. He was eventually caught and executed in 1810. Cf. <en.wikipedia.org/wiki/Adreas_Hofer>, accessed 21 December 2012.

[163] Cf. Dumas, *Histoire d'un casse-noisette*, vol. 1, p. 48; Hoffmann, 'Nussknacker und Mausekönig', p. 131.

[164] Schubert, *La Symbolique du Rêve*, p. 95.

[165] Ibid., p. 100.

[166] Cf. plate no. 12.

[167] Tchaikovsky, *Casse-noisette*, orchestral score, libretto and scenario of Marius Petipa, vol. 2, p. 295.

[168] Theatre Library of St Petersburg, sketches folder 1463/1-20, no. 53.

[169] Tchaikovsky, *Casse-noisette*, piano reduction, p. 64.

[170] Theatre Library of St Petersburg, sketches folder 1463/1-20, no. 18. Cf. plate no. 13.

[171] The Légion d'honneur was established by Napoleon Bonaparte in 1802 as a decoration awarded for merit, regardless of birth. It remains to this day as France's highest decoration.

[172] Tchaikovsky, *Casse-noisette*, orchestral score, libretto and scenario of Marius Petipa, vol. 2, p. 296. The word 'башмачок', meaning 'bootee', is what Claire throws at the Mouse King in the Russian version of the libretto. It must be remembered that, on account of the cold climate, boots were worn indoors in Russia as house boots. The word 'shoe' is used in the French libretto. Petipa in his scenario in French uses the word 'shoe' and 'slipper', and this is also borne out in the Russian translation of Petipa's scenario. Cf. Ibid., p. 299.

[173] Dumas, *Histoire d'un casse-noisette*, vol. 1, p. 93. Cf. plate no. 14.

[174] Cf. Tchaikovsky, *Casse-noisette*, orchestral score, libretto and scenario of Marius Petipa, vol. 2, p. 296.

[175] The shoe in Classical antiquity denoted liberty or freedom, since the slave went barefoot. Cf. Cooper, *An Illustrated Encyclopaedia of Traditional Symbols*, p. 152.

[176] Note that the Bertell etching has rounded toes on Claire's slippers, in keeping with earlier fashions. Cf. plate no. 2.

[177] Schubert, *La Symbolique du Rêve*, p. 73.

[178] Tchaikovsky, *Casse-noisette*, orchestral score, libretto, and scenario of Marius Petipa, vol. 2, p. 296.

[179] Schubert, *La Symbolique du Rêve*, pp. 67-8.

[180] Cf. ibid., p. 158.

[181] Ibid., p. 160.

[182] Ibid., p. 168.

[183] Tchaikovsky, *Casse-noisette*, orchestral score, libretto, and scenario of Marius Petipa, vol. 2, p. 296.

[184] Mikály Hoppál, *Shamans and Traditions* (Budapest, Akadémiai Kiakó, 2007), p. 93.

[185] Cf. *Year Book of the Imperial Theatres* (St Petersburg, 1909), p. 122.

[186] Shamanism, considered a pagan religion, was persecuted under the tsars.

[187] Cf. William Leatherbarrow and Derek Offord (eds.), *A History of Russian Thought* (Cambridge: CUP, 2010), p. 180.

Act I, Scene II

[1] Wiley, *Tchaikovsky's Ballets*, p. 375.

[2] Chevalier and Gheerbrant, *Dictionary of Symbols*, p. 434.

[3] Ibid., p. 1016.

[4] Tchaikovsky, *Casse-noisette*, orchestral score, libretto, and scenario of Marius Petipa, vol. 2, p. 296.

[5] Collection of the Bakhrushin State Theatre Museum, Moscow.

[6] Cf. Hans Biedermann, *Dictionary of Symbolism* (New York: Meridian, 1992), p. 141. Note also that this sequence of events in the story of the ballet contrasts with the texts of Hoffmann and Dumas, where Claire wakes up intermittently from her dream, returning to the reality of her home.

[7] Cf. Cooper, *An Illustrated Encyclopaedia of Traditional Symbols*, p. 71.

[8] Theatre Library of St Petersburg, sketches folder 1463/1-20, no. 21. Cf. plate no. 15.

[9] Tchaikovsky, *Casse-noisette*, orchestral score, libretto and scenario of Marius Petipa, vol. 2, p. 296.

[10] Cf. Tchaikovsky, *Casse-noisette*, piano reduction, pp. 76-91.

[11] Ibid., p. 76.

[12] Tchaikovsky, *Casse-noisette*, orchestral score, vol. 1, p. 285.

[13] Quoted in Wiley, *The Life and Ballets of Lev Ivanov*, p. 140.

[14] Cooper, *An Illustrated Encyclopaedia of Traditional Symbols*, p. 192.

[15] Petipa, in his instructions to Tchaikovsky, points out that the snow-flake scene is to be illuminated by electricity. Cf. Wiley, *Tchaikovsky's Ballets*, p. 374.

[16] Cf. Dumas, *Histoire d'un casse-noisette*, vol. 2, p. 26.

[17] Schubert, *La Symbolique du Rêve*, p. 134.

[18] Ibid., p. 89.

[19] Cf. choreographic score in Stepanov notation of *The Nutcracker*, Harvard Theatre Collection, MS Thr 245. <Pds.lib.harvard.edu/pds/view/45336942>, electronic sequence pages 48-52, accessed 12 March 2014.

[20] For the symbolism of the circle and the sphere, cf. Chevalier and Gheerbrant, *The Penguin Dictionary of Symbols*, pp. 195, 902.

[21] Nikolai Berdyaev, *The Russian Idea* (Hudson, New York: Lindisfarne, 1992), p. 212.

[22] Angela Sumegi, *Dreamworlds of Shamanism and Tibetan Buddhism* (Albany: State University of New York, 2008), p. 27.

[23] Ibid., p. 11.

[24] Cf. ibid., p. 16.

[25] The gingerbread men who *do* die are not spirits in this context, but would be regarded in shamanism as natural phenomena with souls.

[26] Sumegi, *Dreamworlds of Shamanism and Tibetan Buddhism*, p. 18.

Act II

[1] Tchaikovsky, *Casse-noisette*, orchestral score, libretto and scenario of Marius Petipa, vol. 2, p. 299.

[2] Cf. <http://upload.wikimedia.org/wikipedia/commons/f/ff/Nutcracker_set_designs.jpg>, accessed 7 August 2011.

[3] In Buddhism, hemispherical dome-shaped stupas are symbolic of the heavens. Initially spreading northwards from India, Buddhism established itself in China (first century AD), Tibet (fifth century), and Mongolia (sixteenth and seventeenth centuries), as well as other lands. Mongolia became incorporated into Russian territory during the early seventeenth century, and from there Buddhism took root

in Siberia. It is entirely possible that Ivanov drew inspiration for his Confiturembourg designs from pictures of Buddhist architecture within the Russian Empire, brought back to St Petersburg by scientific expeditions.

4   Cf. Biedermann, *Dictionary of Symbolism*, pp. 252, 268.

5   Cooper, *An Illustrated Encyclopaedia of Traditional Symbols*, p. 20.

6   Ibid., p. 19.

7   Cf. Odile Nouvel-Kammerer, *Symbols of Power. Napoleon and the Art of the Empire Style 1800-1815* (Paris: American Federation of the Arts and Les Arts Décoratifs, 2007), p. 167.

8   Ibid., p. 169. Childeric I (*c.* 440-81), King of the Franks.

9   A Leslie Willson, *A Mythical Image: the Ideal of India in German Romanticism* (Durham, NC: Duke University, 1964), p. 84.

10   Cf. ibid., p. 89.

11   Ibid., pp. 121-2.

12   Tchaikovsky, *Casse-noisette*, orchestral score, libretto and scenario of Marius Petipa, vol. 2, p. 299.

13   Theatre Library of St Petersburg, sketches folder 1463/1-20, no. 67. The Sugar Plum Fairy is designated on the sketch in French as 'La Fée Dragée.'

14   Cf. June Campbell, *Traveller in Space: in search of Female Identity in Tibetan Buddhism* (London: Athlone, 1996), p. 116.

15   Cf. Abraham, *A Dictionary of Alchemical Imagery*, pp. 4, 174 and Paul F Cowlan, *The Alchemical Quartet* (Alembic, 2013), p. 74.

16   Tchaikovsky, *Casse-noisette*, orchestral score, libretto and scenario of Marius Petipa, vol. 2, p. 299.

17   Theatre Library of St Petersburg, sketches folder 1463/1-20, nos. 39-46.

18   Ibid., no. 46.

19   Ibid., no. 45.

20   Ibid., no. 44.

21   Abraham, *A Dictionary of Alchemical Imagery*, p. 80.

22   Theatre Library of St Petersburg, sketches folder 1463/1-20, no. 43.

23   Abraham, *A Dictionary of Alchemical Imagery*, p. 120.

24   Alchemical ideas are thought to have spread along the trade routes from the East to Alexandria where they surfaced between the third and fifth centuries AD. From Alexandria they passed into Greek culture.

Cf. Obed Simon Johnson, *A Study of Chinese Alchemy* (Shangai: Commercial Press, 1928), p. 117.

[25] Theatre Library of St Petersburg, sketches folder 1463/1-20, no. 39.

[26] Ibid., no. 40.

[27] Ibid., no. 42. Note that the name of this fairy has been changed in the Russian translated libretto to being a Fairy of 'Dancers'.

[28] Ibid., no. 41.

[29] William Shakespeare, *As You Like It*, Act 2, Scene 7.

[30] Dumas, *Histoire d'un casse-noisette*, vol. 2, p. 101.

[31] Tchaikovsky, *Casse-noisette*, orchestral score, libretto and scenario of Marius Petipa, vol. 2, p. 296.

[32] Theatre Library of St Petersburg, sketches folder 1463/1-20, nos. 58-66.

[33] Ibid., no. 56.

[34] Ibid., no. 57.

[35] Ibid., no. 58.

[36] Ibid., no. 59. Cf. plate no. 16.

[37] The idea for 'Brioche' appears to derive from the Bertell illustration in the Dumas publication of 1845. Cf. Dumas, *Histoire d'un casse-noisette*, vol. 2, p. 97.

[38] Theatre Library of St Petersburg, sketches folder 1463/1-20, no. 60.

[39] Ibid., no. 61.

[40] Ibid., no. 62.

[41] Ibid., no. 63.

[42] Ibid., no. 64.

[43] Ibid., no. 65.

[44] Chevalier and Gheerbrant, *The Penguin Dictionary of Symbols*, p. 842.

[45] Dumas, *Histoire d'un casse-noisette*, vol. 2, p. 101.

[46] Theatre Library of St Petersburg, sketches folder 1463/1-20, no. 66.

[47] Wiley, *The Life and Ballets of Lev Ivanov*, p. 140.

[48] Tchaikovsky, *Casse-noisette*, orchestral score, libretto and scenario of Marius Petipa, vol. 2, p. 299.

[49] Theatre Library of St Petersburg, sketches folder 1463/1-20, no. 90.

[50] Chevalier and Gheerbrant, *The Penguin Dictionary of Symbols*, p. 676.

[51] Cf. plate no. 19. The Bertall illustration from the 1845 publication of *Casse-noisette* by Dumas shows a serene Claire, with the Nutcracker on her knee, gliding along the rosewater river in a shell. The Nutcracker

is still the size of a doll—unlike the ballet at this point, he has not been transformed into a life-sized prince!

52   Tchaikovsky, *Casse-noisette*, orchestral score, libretto and scenario of Marius Petipa, vol. 2, p. 296.

53   Theatre Library of St Petersburg, sketches folder 1463/1-20, no. 91.

54   Cooper, *An Illustrated Encyclopaedia of Traditional Symbols*, p. 182.

55   The hummingbird is found today in the Americas, although the fossil record indicates that it may have existed in southern Russia and China. Cf. <http://en.wikipedia.org/wiki/Hummingbird>, accessed 2 February 2014.

56   In Georgia (annexed by Russia in 1801), honey was, in ancient times, packed up for people's journeys into the afterlife. Cf. <http://en.wikipedia.org/wiki/Honey#In_History.2C_culture.2C_and_folklore>, accessed 1 February 2014.

57   Chevalier and Gheerbrant, *The Penguin Dictionary of Symbols*, p. 511.

58   Cf. Cooper, *An Illustrated Encyclopaedia of Traditional Symbols*, p. 20.

59   Cf. ibid., p. 90.

60   Theatre Library of St Petersburg, sketches folder 1463/1-20, no. 93. The designs specify eight pages in number.

61   Cooper, *An Illustrated Encyclopaedia of Traditional Symbols*, p. 100.

62   Ibid.

63   Theatre Library of St Petersburg, sketches folder 1463/1-20, no. 92.

64   Cf. Tchaikovsky, *Casse-noisette*, orchestral score, libretto and scenario of Marius Petipa, vol. 2, p. 298; and Wiley, *Tchaikovsky's Ballets*, p. 380.

65   Cf. <http://fr.wikipedia.org/wiki/Ang%C3%A9lique_officinale#L.27herbe_aux_anges>, accessed 9 February 2014.

66   Cf. <http://en.wikipedia.org/wiki/Angelica_acutiloba>, accessed 29 June 2012.

67   Theatre Library of St Petersburg, sketches folder 1463/1-20, no. 72.

68   Cf. Cooper, *An Illustrated Encyclopaedia of Traditional Symbols*, p. 40.

69   Cf. Nouvel-Kammerer, *Symbols of Power*, pp. 276-97.

70   Ibid., p. 276.

71   Cf. Cooper, *An Illustrated Encyclopaedia of Traditional Symbols*, p. 75. The symbol of a 'golden flower' refers to an alchemical process, analogous to the opening of a 'golden flower.'

72   Theatre Library of St Petersburg, sketches folder 1463/1-20, no. 73.

73 Cf. Cooper, *An Illustrated Encyclopaedia of Traditional Symbols*, p. 306.
74 Tchaikovsky, *Casse-noisette*, orchestral score, libretto and scenario of Marius Petipa, vol. 2, p. 296.
75 Theatre Library of St Petersburg, sketches folder 1463/1-20, nos. 74, 74 'Variant.'
76 Cf. Cooper, *An Illustrated Encyclopaedia of Traditional Symbols*, pp. 40, 74, 41.
77 Cf. ibid.
78 Mircea Eliade, *The Two and the One*, tr. J M Cohen (London: Harvill, 1965), pp. 43, 45.
79 Tchaikovsky, *Casse-noisette*, orchestral score, libretto and scenario of Marius Petipa, vol. 2, p. 300.
80 Cf. Wiley, *Tchaikovsky's Ballets*, p. 381.
81 Cf. ibid.
82 Quoted in Wiley, *The Life and Ballets of Lev Ivanov*, p. 141.
83 Cf. Joanny Bricaud, 'Le Mysticisme à la Cour de Russie.'
84 Cf. Appendix 1 herein.
85 Tchaikovsky, *Casse-noisette*, orchestral score, libretto and scenario of Marius Petipa, vol. 2, p. 300.
86 Ibid., p. 296.
87 In the Dumas text of *Histoire d'un casse-noisette*, vol. 2, p. 98, there are different peoples included in the throng in Confiturembourg, but they are not Spanish, Arab or Chinese; instead they are: Armenians, Jews, Greeks, Tyroleans, the Great Mogol with seven hundred slaves, and the Grand Sultan accompanied by three hundred janissaries.
88 Theatre Library of St Petersburg, sketches folder 1463/1-20, nos. 94-7.
89 Joseph Bonaparte (1768-1844), as Joesph I, King of Spain (1808-13).
90 Marius Petipa spent the years 1843-6 working in Madrid and is known to have studied this choreographic art form. Cf. <http://en.wikipedia.org/wiki/Marius_Petipa#Madrid>, accessed 5 March 2014.
91 Tchaikovsky, *Casse-noisette*, orchestral score, libretto and scenario of Marius Petipa, vol. 2, p. 301.
92 Theatre Library of St Petersburg, sketches folder 1463/1-20, nos. 87-9.
93 These papers are now in the possession of the Harvard Theatre Collection, Cambridge, Massachusetts. Nicolai Sergeev (1876-1951), Russian repetiteur.

[94] A few dances survive from Sergeev's production of *The Nutcracker* at Sadler's Wells, and they are now preserved in the Benesh archive at the Royal Academy of Dance, London. Benesh notation was introduced at the Sadler's Wells Ballet in the late 1940s and early 1950s by Joan Benesh (1920-2014) and her husband Rudolph Benesh (1916-75), Joan Benesh being a dancer at Sadler's Wells.

[95] Choreographic score in Stepanov notation of *The Nutcracker*, Harvard Theatre Collection, MS Thr 245. Cf. <Pds.lib.harvard.edu/pds/view/45336942>, electronic sequence pp. 90-6, accessed 12 March 2014.

[96] Cooper, *An Illustrated Encyclopaedia of Traditional Symbols*, p. 62.

[97] Ibid., p. 37.

[98] The Stepanov notation does not notate the upper body at this juncture. For the upper body, cf. *Dance Arabe*, Benesh archive, Royal Academy of Dance, London.

[99] Cooper, *An Illustrated Encyclopaedia of Traditional Symbols*, p. 185.

[100] Tchaikovsky, *Casse-noisette*, orchestral score, libretto and scenario of Marius Petipa, vol. 2, p. 301.

[101] In 1789, Russia concluded a treaty on regular tea supplies from China via camel caravan in exchange for furs. Gradually more tea was brought by caravan up until the middle of the nineteenth century when it began to be imported by ship via Odessa and London. Cf. <http://en.wikipedia.org/wiki/Russian_tea_culture>, accessed 9 March 2014.

[102] Ibid.

[103] Theatre Library of St Petersburg, sketches folder 1463/1-20, nos. 98, 101.

[104] Ibid., no. 99.

[105] Ibid., no. 100.

[106] Choreographic score in Stepanov notation of *The Nutcracker*, Harvard Theatre Collection, MS Thr 245. Cf. <Pds.lib.harvard.edu/pds/view/45336942>, electronic sequence pp. 98-104, accessed 12 March 2014.

[107] Collection of the British Film Institute, London.

[108] None of these steps are recorded in the Stepanov notation, with the exception of the arabesque and *relevés*.

[109] Cooper, *An Illustrated Encyclopaedia of Traditional Symbols*, p. 65.

[110] Ibid., p. 182. The staging here of the parasol contrasts with that of the brown umbrella in Act I.

[111] Choreographic score in Stepanov notation of *The Nutcracker*, Harvard Theatre Collection, MS Thr 245. Cf. <Pds.lib.harvard.edu/pds/view/45336942>, electronic sequence p. 104, accessed 12 March 2014.

[112] Cf. Chevalier and Gheerbrant, *The Penguin Dictionary of Symbols*, pp. 61, 738.

[113] Tchaikovsky, *Casse-noisette*, orchestral score, libretto and scenario of Marius Petipa, vol.2, p. 301.

[114] Ibid., p. 296.

[115] Ibid., p. 94.

[116] Apart from the appropriate choice of music, it is not obvious as to why a Ukrainian trepak should have been chosen. Oddly enough, during the Napoleonic invasion of Russia, Ukraine, albeit reluctantly, supplied the French Grand Armée. However, during Napoleon's retreat of 1812, the Ukrainian gentry switched their loyalty back to Russia. Cf. <www.encyclopediaofukraine.com/display.asp?linkpath=pages%5C-N%5CA%5CNapoleonBonaparte.htm>, accessed 23 August 2013.

[117] Quoted in Wiley, *The Life and Ballets of Lev Ivanov*, p. 143. Alexander Shirayev (1867-1941), was a leading Russian character dancer of his time.

[118] Theatre Library of St Petersburg, sketches folder 1463/1-20, no. 75.

[119] <http://en.wikipedia.org/wiki/Jester#The_jester_as_a_symbol>, accessed 14 January 2013, reports that 'In the Middle Ages, Death is often shown in Jester's garb because "The last laugh is reserved for death".'

[120] Tchaikovsky, *Casse-noisette*, orchestral score, libretto and scenario of Marius Petipa, vol. 2, p. 301.

[121] Cf. <fr.wikipedia.org/wiki/Mirliton_(musique)>, accessed 13 January 2013.

[122] Theatre Library of St Petersburg, sketches folder 1463/1-20, no. 71. Cf. plate no. 17.

[123] Ami Ronnberg and Kathleen Martin (eds.), *The Book of Symbols* (Cologne: Taschen, 2010), p. 718.

[124] Cf. recording of 'The Mirlitons' in Benesh notation, Royal Academy of Dance, London, which closely matches the choreographic score in Stepanov notation of *The Nutcracker*, Harvard Theatre Collection, MS Thr 245. Cf. <Pds.lib.harvard.edu/pds/view/45336942>, electronic sequence pp. 104-7, accessed 12 March 2014.

125 Cf. Cooper, *An Illustrated Encyclopaedia of Traditional Symbols*, p. 70.

126 Tchaikovsky, *Casse-noisette*, orchestral score, libretto and scenario of Marius Petipa, vol. 2, p. 301.

127 Cf. Rey and Rey-Debove (eds.), *Le Petit Robert*, p. 866.

128 Theatre Library of St Petersburg, sketches folder 1463/1-20, no. 78.

129 Ibid., no. 76. Usually the traditional Punch wears a black and white mask, signifying life and death, but this is not the case here.

130 The idea of the candy stick finds credence in the fact that 'Mère Gigogne' was 'an identifiable line of bonbons that sold in St Petersburg in 1890. The tin box was in the shape of a woman in a large panniered skirt. The box opened at the bottom of the panniers, and all the little bonbons were inside'. Cf. <http://www.grebeldance.com/NUTCRACKER2008.html>, accessed 26 May 2012.

131 Pierre Louis Duchartre, *The Italian Comedy*, p. 215.

132 Cooper, *An Illustrated Encyclopaedia of Traditional Symbols*, p. 156.

133 Tchaikovsky, *Casse-noisette*, orchestral score, libretto and scenario of Marius Petipa, vol. 2, p. 301. The 'bouquet' in the libretto is described by one critic of the day as 'a large gold vase of golden flowers' (quoted in Wiley, *The Life and Ballets of Lev Ivanov*, p. 144).

134 Cf. Wiley, *Tchaikovsky's Ballets*, p. 381.

135 Theatre Library of St Petersburg, sketches folder 1463/1-20, nos. 69, 70. Cf. plate no. 18.

136 Sunflowers are native to North America. Their seeds were brought back to Europe in the sixteenth century. Their popularization in Russia is credited to Peter the Great and also to the Russian Orthodox Church which did not forbid its consumption as a food during Lent. Cf. <http://www.sunflowernsa.com/all-about/history>, accessed 24 March 2014.

137 Elizabeth Reninger, *The Secret of the Golden Flower*, quoted at <http://taoism.about.com/od/scriptures/qt/goldenflower.htm>, accessed 8 February 2014.

138 Cf. choreographic score in Stepanov notation of *The Nutcracker*, Harvard Theatre Collection, MS Thr 245. Cf. <Pds.lib.harvard.edu/pds/view/45336942>, electronic sequence pp. 108-15, accessed 12 March 2014.

139 *The Secret of the Golden Flower*, tr. Richard Wilhelm (New York: Harcourt Brace, 1962), pp. 21-2.

[140] Ibid., pp. 30-1.

[141] Ibid., p. 40.

[142] Mircea Eliade, *The Two and the One*, p. 48. Mircea Eliade (1907-86), historian and philosopher.

[143] *The Secret of the Golden Flower*, p. 103. Carl Gustav Jung (1875-1961), psychiatrist and psychotherapist.

[144] Tchaikovsky, *Casse-noisette*, orchestral score, libretto and scenario of Marius Petipa, vol. 2, p. 301.

[145] Theatre Library of St Petersburg, sketches folder 1463/1-20, no. 68. Cf. plate no. 21.

[146] Rey and Rey-Debove (eds.), *Le Petit Robert*, p. 391.

[147] Theatre Library of St Petersburg, sketches folder 1463/1-20, no. 68. Cf. plate no. 21.

[148] Feng shui philosophy is a system of harmonizing human existence with the surrounding environment. Colours symbolizing the five elements can vary slightly. Cf. <http://en.wikipedia.org/wiki/Feng_shui>, accessed 27 March 2014; and <fengshui.about.com/od/thebasics/qt/fiveelements.htm>, accessed 5 April 2013.

[149] Cooper, *An Illustrated Encyclopaedia of Traditional Symbols*, p. 184.

[150] Ibid., p. 163.

[151] Cf. Wiley, *Tchaikovsky's Ballets*, p. 381.

[152] Cooper, *An Illustrated Encyclopaedia of Traditional Symbols*, p. 128. This attribution ties in with the pearls on the costumes for the Waltz of the Flowers as the crystallization of light circulation. And indeed, the idea of circulation is picked up in the round necklaces and pearled armhole surrounds. Cf. plate nos. 21, 22.

[153] Cf. Choreographic score in Benesh notation of *The Nutcracker Pas de Deux*, Benesh archive, Royal Academy of Dance, London. Cf. Choreographic score in Stepanov notation of *The Nutcracker*, Harvard Theatre Collection, MS Thr 245. Cf. <Pds.lib.harvard.edu/pds/view/45336942>, electronic sequence pp. 155-9, accessed 12 March 2014.

[154] Cooper, *An Illustrated Encyclopaedia of Traditional Symbols*, p. 96.

[155] Cf. Chevalier and Gheerbrant, *Dictionary of Symbols*, p. 621. In China, the lozenge is also (less applicable here) an important symbol of victory.

[156] This phrase has been cut from the Benesh record.

157 Wiley, *Tchaikovsky's Ballets*, p. 219. Vavara Alexandrovna Nikitina (1857-1920) and Pavel Andreyevich Gerdt (1844-1917), dancers of the Imperial Ballet, St Petersburg. Roland John Wiley (b. 1942), American musicologist. Cf. plate no. 22.

158 Choreographic score in Stepanov notation of *The Nutcracker*, Harvard Theatre Collection, MS Thr 245. Cf. <Pds.lib.harvard.edu/pds/view/45336942>, electronic sequence p. 159, plan 3, accessed 12 March 2014.

159 Cf. Cooper, *An Illustrated Encyclopaedia of Traditional Symbols*, p. 184.

160 A celesta is a keyboard instrument in the form of an upright piano invented by Auguste Mustel in 1866. It was therefore a relative novelty at the time of its inclusion in *The Nutcracker*. The sound of the celesta is similar to a glockenspiel, but much softer, and more celestial in its tone, a quality which gave the instrument its name.

161 Choreographic score in Stepanov notation of *The Nutcracker*, Harvard Theatre Collection, MS Thr 245. Cf. <Pds.lib.harvard.edu/pds/view/45336942>, electronic sequence pp. 163-5, accessed 12 March 2014. Cf. choreographic fragment in Benesh notation from *The Nutcracker*, Benesh archive, Royal Academy of Dance, London.

162 '*Caractère*' is movement outside the classical vocabulary, which can be taken as representative of a certain type of 'character'. Here the 'character' is that of scattering and planting seeds. Where arm movements blend with classical steps, the combination is known as '*demi-caractère*'.

163 Cf. plate no. 20.

164 Cf. <Pds.lib.harvard.edu/pds/view/45336942>, electronic sequence pp. 163-5, accessed 12 March 2014.

165 Tchaikovsky, *Casse-noisette*, orchestral score, libretto and scenario of Marius Petipa, vol. 2, p. 301.

166 Ibid., p. 296.

167 Ibid., p. 301.

168 Ibid., p. 296.

Conclusion

1 Lesley Chamberlain, *Motherland. A Philosophical History of Russia* (London: Atlantic Books, 2004), pp. 43-4.

2   Ibid., p. 121.

3   Ibid., p. 122.

4   Ibid.

5   Wiley, *Tchaikovsky's Ballets*, p. 220. There is no costume design for the student bees in Vsevolojsky's original costume sketches. Maybe costumes already existed in the theatre wardrobe which obviated the need to create a new design.

6   Shlapentokh, *The French Revolution in Russian Intellectual Life 1865-1905* (New Brunswick, NJ: Transaction Punlishers, 2009), p. 83.

7   Ibid., p. 86.

8   Ibid., pp. 86-7.

9   Ibid., p. 88.

10   Maxim Maksimovich Kovalevsky (1851-1916), Russian sociologist.

11   Shlapentokh, *The French Revolution in Russian Intellectual Life 1865-1905*, p. 88.

12   Andrzej Walicki, *A History of Russian Thought: From the Enlightenment to Marxism* (Stanford, California: Stanford University Press, 1979), pp. 367-8.

13   Napoleon's Continental Blockade was an embargo against British trade after the British set up a naval blockade of the French coasts in 1806. By the Berlin Decree of 1806, Napoleon, in response, banned all trade with Britain by France and its allies. However, British control of the oceans ensured that more economic damage befell Napoleon and his allies: goods like tea, coffee and chocolate, which relied upon ocean shipment would have been affected and would have become more difficult to import into Continental Europe until the blockade was lifted.

14   Shlapentokh, *The French Revolution in Russian Intellectual Life 1865-1905*, p. 92.

15   Ibid., p. 93.

16   Vsevolojsky was appointed to his post of Director of the Imperial Theatres by Alexander III, Russian tsar (1881-1894).

17   Chamberlain, *Motherland. A Philosophical History of Russia*, p. 85. Roman Osipovich Jakobson (1892-1982), Russian philologist.

18   The more revolutionary ideas of the radicals took on a more aggressive stance at the beginning of the twentieth century. Cf. Shlapentokh, *The French Revolution in Russian Intellectual Life 1865-1905*, pp. 101-46.

Appendix I

1   Cynthia H Whittaker, *The Origins of Modern Russian Education: an Intellectual Biography of Count Sergei Uvarov 1786-1855* (De Kalb, IL: Northern Illinois University, 1984), p. 20.

2   Peter I (the Great), Tsar of Russia 1689-1725. Catherine II (the Great), Tsarina of Russia 1762-1796, was to follow Peter's policies.

3   Cf. Whittaker, *The Origins of Modern Russian Education*, p. 20.

4   Cf. Andrei A Znamenski, *The Beauty of the Primitve. Shamanism and the Western Imagination* (Oxford: OUP, 2007), p. 5.

5   Karl Wilhelm Friedrich Schlegel (1772-1829), German scholar and leader of German Romanticism. He, along with his brother August, published a periodical in Berlin from 1798 to 1800, called the *Athenäum*, in which theorists of the Romantic movement outlined the principles which were to guide the Romantic poets.

6   Znamenski, *The Beauty of the Primitive. Shamanism and the Western Imagination*, p. 14.

7   Johann Gottfried Herder (1744-1803), German philosopher.

8   Znamenski, *The Beauty of the Primitve. Shamanism and the Western Imagination*, p. 23.

9   Friedrich Wilhelm Joseph Schelling (1775-1854), German philosopher and writer. Cf. Willson, *A Mythical Image: the Ideal of India in German Romanticism*, pp. 114-17.

10 Cf. Berdyaev, *The Russian Idea*, p. 49.

11 Schelling published his ideas about nature in *Ideen zu einer Philosophie der Natur* (*Ideas concerning a Philosophy of Nature*) in 1797.

12 Cf. Willson, *A Mythical Image: the Ideal of India in German Romanticism*, pp. 121-3.

13 Schubert, *La Symbolique du Rêve*, p. 82.

14 Ibid., p. 92.

15 Peter Furst quoted in Sumegi, *Dreamworlds of Shamanism and Tibetan Buddhism*, p. 12.

16 Fyodor Golubinsky (1797-1854), Russian philosophical theologian.

17 Cf. Norman W Ingham, *E.T.A. Hoffmann's Reception in Russia* (Würzburg: jal-verlag, 1974), p. 9.

18 Ibid., p. 243.

19 The city of Kazan lies at the confluence of the rivers Volga and

Kazanka, 500 miles east of Moscow and around 500 miles west of the
Ural mountains.

20 Count Sergei Uvarov (1786-1855), Russian intellectual and orientalist.
One of his main influences was Schlegel.

21 Cf. Whittaker, *The Origins of Modern Russian Education*, p. 22.

22 Ibid., p. 21.

23 Vasilii Grigor'ev (1816-81), Russian orientologist. N.B. that Vsevolojsky,
attended the University of St Petersburg during this period and may
well have been influenced by developments there.

24 Cf. Vera Tolz, *Russia's Own Orient* (Oxford: OUP, 2011), pp. 8-9.

25 Cf. Peter Shamimov, 'Leibniz and the Russian Philosophy in the 19th
and 20th Century', in *Leibniz und Europa. VI Internationaler Leibniz-
Kongreß* (Langenhagen, 1994), p. 745. Gottfried Wilhelm Leibniz
(1646-1716), German philosopher.

26 Victor Romanovich Rozen (1849-1908), Russian orientalist and acade-
mician of the St Petersburg Academy of Sciences.

27 Tolz, *Russia's Own Orient*, p. 9.

28 Friedrich Wilhelm Radloff (1837-1918).

29 Barnaul is situated relatively close to Kazakhstan, Mongolia and China.

30 Cf. <en.wikipedia.org/wiki/Trans-Siberian_Railway>, accessed 26
December 2013.

Bibliography

Manuscripts and Other Primary Material

Benesh Institute Archive, Library of the Royal Academy of Dance, London.

Unpublished choreographic fragments from *The Nutcracker*, notated by Joan Benesh et al.

State Theatre Library of St Petersburg.

Ivan Vsevolojsky's Sketches of Costumes for The Nutcracker, inventory no. 1463/1-20.

Published Works

Abraham, Lyndy, *A Dictionary of Alchemical Imagery* (Cambridge: CUP, 1998).

Au temps des Merveilleuses: La Société parisienne sous le Directoire et le Consulat (Paris: Musée Carnavalet, 2005).

Berdyaev, Nikolai, *The Russian Idea* (Hudson, New York: Lindisfarne, 1992).

Biedermann, Hans, *Dictionary of Symbolism* (New York: Meridian, 1992).

Campbell, June, *Traveller in Space: in search of Female Identity in Tibetan Buddhism* (London: Athlone, 1996).

Carlson, Maria, *No Religion Higher than Truth. A History of the Theosophical Movement in Russia, 1875-1922* (Princeton, New Jersey: Princeton University, 1993).

Chamberlain, Lesley, *Motherland. A Philosophical History of Russia* (London: Atlantic Books, 2004).

Chevalier, Jean and Gheerbrant, Alain, *Dictionary of Symbols* (London: Penguin, 1996).

Cirlot, J E, *A Dictionary of Symbols* (Mineola, New York: Dover, 2002).

Clayton, J Douglas, *'Pierrot' in Petrograd* (Montreal: McGill-Queen's University, 1993).

Cooper, J C, *An Illustrated Encyclopaedia of Traditional Symbols* (London: Thames & Hudson, 1978).

Clark, William, Golinski, Jan, and Schaffer, Simon (eds.), *The Sciences in Enlightened Europe* (London: University of Chicago, 1999).

Ducharte, Pierre Louis, *The Italian Comedy* (New York: Dover, 1966).

Dumas, Alexandre, *Histoire d'un casse-noisette* (Paris: J Hetzel, 1845).

Ferguson, George, *Signs and Symbols in Christian Art* (Oxford: OUP, 1961).

Folkard, Richard, *Plant Lore, Legends and Lyrics* (London: Sampson Low & Co., 1884).

Gill, John H, *With Eagles to Glory* (London: Greenhill, 1992).

Girard, Victor, *La Transmigration des Ames* (Paris: Perrin, 1888).

Hoffmann, E T A, 'Nussknacker und Mausekönig', in *Kinder-Mährchen* (Berlin: 1816).

Hoppál, Mikály, *Shamans and Traditions* (Budapest, Akadémiai Kiakó, 2007).

Johnson, Obed Simon, *A Study of Chinese Alchemy* (Shangai: Commercial Press, 1928).

Ingham, Norman, W, *E.T.A. Hoffmann's Reception in Russia* (Würzburg: jal-verlag, 1974).

Kilcher, Andreas B and Thiesohn, Philipp (eds.), *Die Enzyklopädik des Esoterik* (München: Wilhelm Fink, 2010).

La Mettrie, Julien Offray de, *Man a Machine* (La Salle, IL: Open Court, 1912).

Leatherbarrow, William and Offord, Derek (eds.), *A History of Russian Thought* (Cambridge: CUP, 2010).

Millington, Thomas Street, *A Lecture on the Phenomena of Dreams, Mesmerism, Clairvoyance* (London: Bailliere, 1852).

Eliade, Mircea, *The Two and the One* (London: Harvill, 1965).

Nouvel-Kammerer, Odile, *Symbols of Power. Napoleon and the Art of the Empire Style 1800-1815* (Paris: American Federation of Arts and Les Arts Décoratifs, 2007).

Outram, Dorinda, *Panorama of the Enlightenment* (Los Angeles: J Paul Getty Museum, 2006).

Philpot, J H, *The Sacred Tree* (London: Macmillan, 1897).

Rey, A and J Rey-Debove (eds.), *Le Petit Robert* (Paris: Dictionnaires LE ROBERT, 1991).

Ronnberg, Ami and Kathleen Martin (eds.), *The Book of Symbols* (Cologne: Taschen, 2010).

Rowland, Beryl, *Birds with Human Souls* (Knoxville: University of Tennessee, 1978).

Savill, Rosalind, *The Wallace Collection. French Gold Boxes* (London: Wallace Collection, 1991).

Shlapentokh, Dmitry, *The French Revolution in Russian Intellectual Life 1865-1905* (New Brunswick, NJ: Transaction Publishers, 2009).

Schneid, Frederick C, *Soldiers of Napoleon's Kingdom of Italy* (Oxford: Westview, 1995).

Schubert, Gotthilf Heinrich, *La Symbolique du Rêve* (Paris: Albin Michel, 1982).

Sumegi, Angela, *Dreamworlds of Shamanism and Tibetan Buddhism* (Albany: State University of New York, 2008).

Tchaikovsky, Peter, *Casse-noisette*, piano reduction (Moscow: P Jurgenson, 1892).

———, *Casse-noisette*, orchestral score, libretto and, scenario of Marius Petipa (Moscow: State Music Publishing, 1955).

Tolz, Vera, *Russia's Own Orient* (Oxford: OUP, 2011).

Walicki, Andrzej, *A History of Russian Thought: From the Enlightenment to Marxism* (Stanford, CA: Stanford University Press, 1979).

Whittaker, Cynthia H, *The Origins of Modern Russian Education: an Intellectual Biography of Count Sergei Uvarov 1786-1855* (De Kalb, IL: Northern Illinois University, 1984).

Wilhelm, Richard (tr.), *The Secret of the Golden Flower* (New York: Harcourt Brace, 1962).

Wiley, Roland John, *The Life and Ballets of Lev Ivanov* (Oxford: Clarendon, 1997).

———, *Tchaikovsky's Ballets. Swan Lake, Sleeping Beauty, Nutcracker* (Oxford: Clarendon, 1985).

Willson, A Leslie, *A Mythical Image: the Ideal of India in German*

Romanticism (Durham, NC: Duke University, 1964).

Znamenski, Andrei A, *The Beauty of the Primitve. Shamanism and the Western Imagination* (Oxford: OUP, 2007).

Index

Scots pines, 62
seeds, 29. 65, 74, 82, 103-4; (sow-
ing of), 106-9
Sergeev, Nicolai, 88, 105
shamanism, 51-2, 57-9, 120, 124
Shiryaev, Alexander, 93
shoe, 15, 48-9, 84
Siberia, 51, 124
Silberhaus, house of silver, 6, 36
Silberhauses, the, 9-11; see also
plate no. 2
silver, *see* moonlight
silver soldiers, 76-7; see also plate
no. 24
sisters of the Nutcracker Prince, 82-4
The Sleeping Beauty, 98, 100
slipper, *see* shoe
snowflakes, 54-5, 57, 59; see also
plate no. 15
snowstorm, *see* whirlwind
Soldier doll, 21-3
Spain (Napoleonic), 86
Spanish dance, 85-7
sphere, 48, 57, 66, 91, 93-4
spiral, 94-5, 97
spirit forces, *see* shamanism
stars (golden), 68, 103
Stepanov notation recordings, 11,
19, 88, 92, 98, 100, 104-6, 108
stupa, 61
Sucre d'Orge, *see* Barley Sugar
Sugar Plum Fairy, 64-6, 71-2, 75,
82, 102-8, 115; see also plate
nos. 20, 22; (suite of), 66-70, 77
sun (as symbol), 8, 24, 66-8, 78-9,
83, 92, 94

sunflowers, 99-100
Sutler doll, 21-3; see also plate
no. 6
sweetmeats, 7, 14, 61, 71-7
Sweets, Kingdom of, *see* Confiturembourg
La Symbolique du Rêve, 39, 46, 57
symbolism of the occult, *see* occult
symbolism

Taoism, 81, 99
Tchaikovsky, Peter, vii, 1, 20, 53,
86-7, 93
tea, 85-6, 90-3; (in Russia), 90
Tibet, 62, 83
time (notion of), 12, 38, 40, 51, 55
tin soldiers, 47
torches, *see* gnomes
transformation, *see* journey
transmigration of the soul, *see*
metempsychosis
Trans-Siberian Railway, 124
tree (climbing the), 51-2
Tree of Death, 43
Tree of Light, 12
trepak, 93
turbulence, 55
Tyrol, 45

Ukraine, 93
umbrella (brown), 10-11
underworld, 43, 48, 53
Uvarov, Count Sergei, 122

veil, *see* Arabian dance
veil of illusion, the, 103, 106